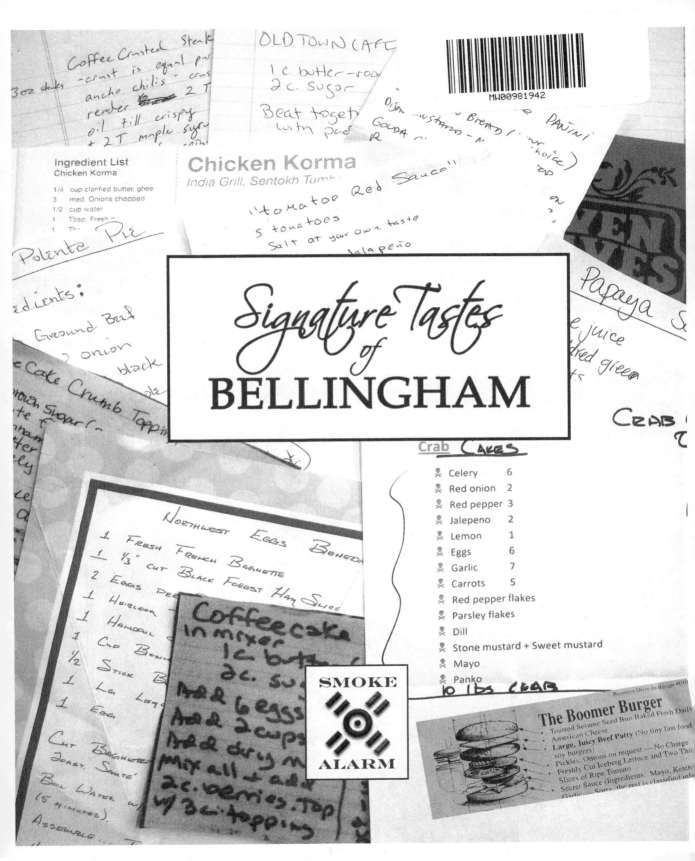

To Karen...it took until I was this age because you were damn hard to find.

Welcome to Bellingham: City of Subdued Excitement photography graciously provided by the encyclopedic talents of Jeff Jewell, Whatcom Museum of History and Art. The most excellent prose was compiled by the rabidly efficient Jacqueline Cartier of the Bellingham/Whatcom County Visitor's Bureau.

An incredible "Thank you" to Michael Golden for the great market photo on the back cover and on the Bellingham Farmer's Market page. You are a very talented photographer.

Back cover quote of Ryan Stiles from Bill Purpura, editor of the Ohio edition of AAA's Home and Away magazine, as submitted by Laurie Peterson.

To Jennifer Slinger, continued international text tech support and a newfound belief that Canadians have the right idea on so many different levels.

To Kulshan.com for insights into our home and area.

To others unnamed, because my memory is as short as my hair.

Layout by Karen G. New and Steven W. Siler

Photography by Steven W. Siler except where noted.

Moral support by Karen G. New, Joey the Labradoodle, and a host of family, friends and fire-fighters. You, not a map, define where home is.

Library of Congress Control Number: 2010914016

Siler, Steven W.

   Signature Tastes of Bellingham: The Favorite Recipes of our Local Kitchens

   ISBN 978-0-9867155-0-1

   1. Restaurants-Washington-Bellingham-Guidebooks. 2. Cookery-Washington-Bellingham.

Printed in the United States of America

This book is dedicated to the emergency responders...

From the first frantic call to Prospect
To the comforting hands at St. Joe's.
You give your time...

away from spouses,
away from friends,
away from children,
And yes, even from meals...

To assure all of us:

"Tonight, I will make it better for you
no matter what,
I will watch over you..."

I have always wondered if anyone really reads the Table of Contents. Now since this is a cookbook, I should have organized everything under its proper heading, like soups, pasta, desserts and the like. Well, we are in Bellingham now, and we don't always do everything the way others do it. This is not just a cookbook as much as a guidebook; a celebration of the city itself...about the eateries, fine dining, casual dining, bars, drive -ins, and of course, the people.

CITY OF SUBDUED EXCITEMENT

"Oh Bellingham!" A refrain often heard from long-time denizens and visitors alike to the northernmost city of the Pacific Northwest. On the shores of Bellingham Bay with Mount Baker as its backdrop, Bellingham is the last major city before the Washington coastline meets the Canadian border. But to understand Bellingham, really understand her, you have to dig. It's rather like looking for clams in the mud flats of Taylor Shellfish. Because Bellingham does not readily yield her true identity, nor can she be pigeon-holed into one category. Unless of course "uniquely-picturesque-artsy-nature loving-proudly local-stunning vistas-laid back-progressive-biking-kayaking-historical-welcoming-City of Subdued Excitement" is a category!

The name of Bellingham is derived from the bay on which the city is situated. George Vancouver, who visited the area in June of 1792, named the bay for Sir William Bellingham, the controller of the storekeeper's account of the Royal Navy. Nature was generous to Whatcom County of which Bellingham serves as the county seat. One can enjoy enchanting views of the area's snowy peaks, lively salt and fresh water shorelines, and expansive evergreen forests with dramatic backdrops. Even within the State of Washington, the area is unique. Temperate weather not even found a few miles south or east combines with magnificent natural scenery, skiing, snowboarding, hiking, biking, water activities (including whale watching!), arts, charming villages, history, and of course, great food!

Replica of George Vancouver's ship
Pacific Swift

JACQUELINE CARTIER , BELLINGHAM/WHATCOM COUNTY TOURISM

WELCOME TO BELLINGHAM

Long before the first Euro-settlers came to this area, Bellingham was home to two Coast Salish Native Tribes: the Lummis of Lummi Peninsula and the Nooksack tribe that lived up river. Like many of us who wish they could do the same, the native populations lived off the fish and shellfish of this area. The first European settlers were led to the bay in canoes by Lummis who also helped clear the land and build the first buildings here, providing food and helping them survive their first winter here.

The first white settlers reached the area in 1854. In 1858, the Fraser Canyon Gold Rush caused thousands of miners, storekeepers, and scalawags to head north from California. Whatcom grew overnight from a small northwest mill town to a bustling seaport, the base town for the Whatcom Trail, which led to the Fraser Canyon goldfields, used in open defiance of colonial Governor James Douglas's edict that all entry to the gold colony be made via Victoria, British Columbia in Canada.

Coal mining occurred in the Bellingham for over a century, from the city's founding in the 1850's until the 1950's. Coal was originally discovered by Henry Roeder off the northeastern shore of Bellingham Bay. In 1854, a group of San Francisco investors established Bellingham Bay Coal Company. The mine extended to hundreds of miles of tunnels as deep as 1,200 feet. It ran southwest to Bellingham Bay, on both sides of Squalicum Creek, an area of about one square mile. It employed some 250 miners digging over 200,000 tons of coal annually, at its peak in the 1920s. It was

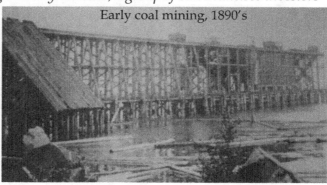

Early coal mining, 1890's

closed in 1955. Even today, the train that serviced the mines lies at the deep bottom of Lake Whatcom, pushed off the rails that once lined the lake.

8

CITY OF SUBDUED EXCITEMENT

The culinary tastes of this time might be hard to recognize by today's standards. Local game was prolific, and frequently appeared on the offerings of menus of the day. One familiar similarity to today, however, was the presence of food with alcohol. Early tavern owners, like modern times, realized patrons would drink more (the profitable side of the business) if they were able to eat as well. So out came the prepared foods for both hungry and thirsty customers alike. And with echoes to prepared foods today, be assured that there was a liberal amount of salt in the food, to encourage those parched throats to quench with a lusty lager.

Bellingham saloon, c. 1905

In 1890, Fairhaven developers bought Bellingham. Whatcom and Sehome had adjacent borders and both towns wanted to merge; thus they formed New Whatcom. Later on October 27, 1903, the word "New" was dropped from the name, because the Washington State legislature outlawed the word "NEW" from city names, making it into simply "Whatcom". If you look, there are no towns in Washington with a name that starts with "NEW". At first, attempts to combine Fairhaven and Whatcom failed, and there was controversy over the name of the proposed new city. Whatcom citizens wouldn't support a city named "Fairhaven", and Fairhaven residents wouldn't support a city named "Whatcom". They eventually decided to use the name "Bellingham", which remains today.

In the early 1890s, three railroad lines arrived, connecting the bay cities to a nation-wide market of builders. The foothills around Bellingham were clear-cut after the 1906 San Francisco earthquake to help provide the lumber for the rebuilding of San Francisco. In 1891, Railroad Avenue was the scene of one of the most bizarre incidents in Bellingham history. Bellingham hoped its Bellingham Bay and British Columbia Railroad (BB&BC) would hook up to the Canadian Pacific Railroad to the north. A regular Canadian Pacific run from Bellingham to Canada would be an economic coupe for the city.

Bellingham train, 1920's

A trial run, the first overland Canadian Pacific train on the BB&BC line, arrived in Bellingham on June 22. The festivities did not go as planned.

Several thousand locals were present for the big affair and awaited the arrival of many Canadian dignitaries on the incoming train. Besides a "Welcome Railway" arch built across the tracks, Bellingham Bay's volunteer fire departments planned to provide an arch of water for the train to travel under, supplied by fire hoses on each side of the train. Over-excitement (or too much drink) led one brigade to shoot off their hose prematurely, as a result, the other brigade was drenched. Not to be outdone, the second company fought back. In the uproar, the incoming train and its distinguished passengers were forgotten. By the time it came in, a full-fledged water fight was underway across the tracks. The much-surprised Canadian Pacific dignitaries on the train, in their finest formal wear, were soaked through the open windows of their cars.

To add insult to injury, reveling crowds observed that the Canadian flag on the arch reached higher than the American flags. Ladders went up, down came the flag, and to the horror of the Canadian guests, their flag was trampled. Officials from both sides of the border were aghast, and formal apologies were tendered. Many old-timers claimed the famous water fight resulted in the cancellation of the rumored purchase of the BB&BC by the Canadian Pacific. The guilty volunteer firefighters? None other than precedents of the author's own South Whatcom Fire Authority!

CITY OF SUBDUED EXCITEMENT

Bellingham was officially incorporated on November 4, 1903 as a result of the incremental consolidation of four towns initially situated around Bellingham Bay during the final decades of the 19th Century. Whatcom is today's "Old Town" area and was founded in 1852. Sehome was an area downtown founded in 1854. Bellingham was further south near Boulevard Park, founded in 1853; while Fairhaven was a large commercial district with its own harbor, also founded in 1853.

W.H. Giles at 511 W. Holly, c. 1910

Even early on, Bellingham was developing its own "Signature Tastes", in products known throughout the whole of North America at the time. Bellingham's proximity to the Strait of Juan de Fuca and to the Inside Passage to Alaska helped keep some cannery operations here. P.A.F., for example, shipped empty cans to Alaska, where they were packed with fish and shipped back for storage. At one time, Bellingham was home to the World's Largest Salmon Cannery, at a time when salmon was truly "King".

Samples of canned salmon from Bellingham

Bellingham is the hub of a robust local and regional economy and home to a diverse business community featuring large and small companies across many sectors. Major employers in Whatcom County represent about 25% of the total jobs in the county. The city encourages small business development and as a result, these businesses make up the largest percent-age of Bellingham's employment. Bellingham and the surrounding county have also gained a national reputation for commitment to local sustainability. Whatcom County represents a growing community of businesses, government entities, schools and

Restaurant delivery trucks, 1955

families who are dedicated to going green, buying local, and reducing waste. The community encourages the exploration, enjoyment and protection of the outdoors and wildlife. Every one of the contributors to this book is a Bellingham business, and form the economic backbone of the city!

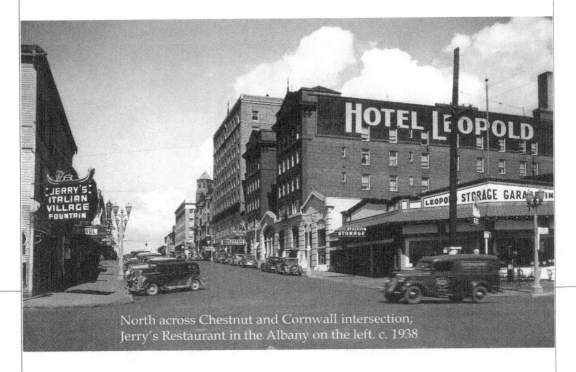

North across Chestnut and Cornwall intersection;
Jerry's Restaurant in the Albany on the left. c. 1938

MICHIGAN HOME RESTAURANT

JOHN BROWNELL, PROP.

SHORT ORDER BILL OF FARE

CEREALS

Germea, with Cream............10	Boiled Rice, with Cream.......10
Oatmeal, with Milk...........5	Cornmeal, with Cream.........10
Oatmeal, with Cream..........10	

Coffee, Tea, Chocolate or Milk, with Cereals, 5 cents extra

TOASTS

Boston Cream Toast...........15	Dry Toast....................5
Dip Toast....................10	Buttered Toast...............10
French Toast.................20	Milk Toast...................10

Coffee, Tea, Chocolate or Milk, with Toasts, 5 cents extra

HOT CAKES

German Pancake..............25	Potato Cakes.................15
Buckwheat Cakes.............10	Cornmeal Cakes...............10
Flannel Cakes................10	

STEAKS AND CHOPS

Plain Steak..................25	Mutton Chops.................25
Hamburg Steak...............25	Lamb Chops..................25
Sirloin Steak................35	Pork Chops...................25
Tenderloin Steak............40	Veal Cutlets.................25
Porterhouse Steak...........45	Veal Cutlets, breaded.........30
Family Porterhouse, for two...75	Ham and Eggs.................25
Liver and Bacon.............25	Bacon and Eggs...............25
Liver and Onions.............25	Pork Sausage.................25

Coffee, Tea or Milk free, with Meat or Egg orders

EGGS AND OMELETS

Three Eggs, fried boiled, scrambled or poached.............25	Plain Omelets................25
	Ham Omelets.................25
Three Eggs, poached on toast...25	Spanish Omelets..............30
Three Eggs, shirred...........25	Rum Omelets.................35

OYSTERS

Raw, per plate...............25	Pepper Roast.................35
Stew........................30	Fancy Pan Roast..............35
Fried.......................35	Oyster Loaf..................50
Pan Roast...................35	Oyster Omelet...............50

EXTRAS

Codfish Cakes................15	French Peas..................20
Potato Salad.................10	Cream Gravy.................10
Lobster Salad................25	Fried Onions.................10
Chicken Salad................25	Russian Caviar...............25
Chicken Salad Spanish........25	Cake and Coffee..............10
Mushrooms..................20	Canned Corn.................10

FISH

Norwegian (Imp.) Mackerel.....25	Norwegian (Imp.) Herring.....25
Salmon......................25	Smelt.......................25
Halibut.....................25	Trout.......................35

EDSON & IRISH, PRINTERS, WHATCOM

May 23, 1902 *# 4875*

Bellingham restaurant "Michigan Home" 1902.
Note that Salmon is the same price as three
scrambled eggs. Prices are in cents.

Some favorite activities to enjoy...

- Challenge your mind at the renowned Whatcom Museum and the Lightcatcher Building. Bring the kids to the FIG (Family Interactive Gallery) for innovative, interactive, green-friendly fun. See exhibits of inventions and innovations that changed the course of history at the one-of-a-kind American Museum of Radio and Electricity

- Embark on a soft adventure hike through fresh mountain meadows or along lakes and seashores. Visit local parks like the waterfront Boulevard Park in Bellingham or Hovander Park in Ferndale to feed the geese and rabbits

- Tour Bellingham's growing waterfront, featuring an eclectic mix of restaurants, high-end shops, parks, promenades, whale watching charters and luxurious lodging

- Discover historic Fairhaven, explore Victorian buildings that host upscale shops and some of Bellingham's finest restaurants

- Sit back, relax and take in a show at the Mt. Baker Theatre or Western Washington University Performing Arts Center

- Enjoy year-round gallery art walks in downtown Bellingham and Fairhaven

- Pamper yourself at the luxurious Semiahmoo Resort, Hotel Bellwether, Chrysalis Inn & Spa or Silver Reef Hotel, Casino and Spa

- Watch windmills turn in Lynden. Shop at the many authentic Dutch shops, entertaining festivals and the Lynden Pioneer Museum

- Compete in one of several epic county-wide races, like Ski to Sea, Bellingham Traverse or Tour de Whatcom

- Sample culinary and agri-tourism delights in a farm-to-fork network that includes local

Bellingham was pet friendly even in 1957. Mrs. Ethel LeCocq and Bambi enjoying a cup of coffee.

farms, wine tours, excellent restaurants, and artisan venues. Taste world-class coffee, hazelnuts, wine and beer, cheeses, apples, ice cream, berries, chocolates, seafood and more.

CITY OF SUBDUED EXCITEMENT

Bellingham's Culinary Delights

Given the pride of the city, it is easy to understand why local food and sustainable farming are key ingredients of the social culture in Bellingham. Whatcom County is a robust mix of gourmet chefs, local growers and savvy eaters all dedicated to preserving and celebrating their unique cultural "food-shed." Locals enjoy handcrafted artisan cheeses, chocolate truffles and local wines. The Bellingham-Mt. Baker region is home to a thriving network of farms and fisheries, which supply the community with a wide variety of locally harvested products.

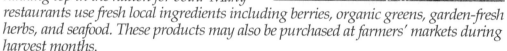

The physical beauty of the region has also attracted talented chefs eager to tailor their skills to the regional harvest. Wild salmon, shellfish, buffalo, lavender, artisan cheeses, gourmet chocolates, award-winning wine and microbrews are all highlights here. Agriculturally, Whatcom County is especially prolific in raspberry and dairy production, ranking top in the nation for both. Many restaurants use fresh local ingredients including berries, organic greens, garden-fresh herbs, and seafood. These products may also be purchased at farmers' markets during harvest months.

Accolades & Fun Facts -- Food for Thought

- *Espresso Capital:* What-com County holds the record for the most drive-up espresso stands per-capita in Washington. More than 50 stands dot the landscape, with such lively names as "I Wanna Moka" and "Shot in the Dark."

- *America's Raspberry Capital:* Whatcom County is the largest pro-ducer of red raspberries in the nation, harvesting more than 57 million pounds each year. This represents al-most 65% of the raspberries grown in the nation. Most of the raspberries are shipped to Ocean Spray and Smuckers and used in making their juices and jams.

- *Shellfish & Clams:* The Taylor Shellfish Farm, located off scenic Chuckanut Drive, is the largest Manila clam producer in the United States and cultivates a greater variety of shellfish than any other shellfish grower in the nation. Taylor Shell-fish Farm has been farming the tidelands along Chuckanut Drive since 1890 and sells fresh oys-ters, clams, mussels, crab, scallops and prawns on site.

Chuckanut Shell, 1948

- *Got Powdered Milk?* Whatcom County is #1 in the nation in milk production per cow, producing more than 1.3 billion pounds of milk each year, and the largest producer of powdered milk. Each day, four million pounds of fluid milk (about 480,000 gallons) come into the Darigold Plant in Lynden, which equates to 53 double tanker truck loads per day. The fluid milk is then converted into 400,000 pounds of powdered milk.

- *Best Place To Drink Wine:* Gadling.com named Bellingham "One of the 25 Greatest Cities in the World for Drinking Wine," noting the city's wine bars, local wine, proximity to British Co-lumbia and laid-back pace of life.

Tulip Festival Parade, the restaurants' float, 1925

HUCKLEBERRY SLUMP

Located on Squalicum Harbor in Bellwether on the Bay, Anthony's Hearthfire Grill presents guests with spectacular views of Bellingham Bay and the San Juan Islands. Offering guests premier Northwest designer beef, this high-energy restaurant specializes in hearthfire cooking. Our menu features fresh Northwest designer beef and seafood including Northwest favorites such as yellowfin ahi tuna steak.

Berry Filling:
3 lbs Northwest huckleberries*
1 tbsp cornstarch
¾ cup granulated sugar

Topping:
1 cup flour, self rising
⅔ cup sugar
5 tbsp unsalted butter, cold
1 cup whipping cream
1 pint vanilla ice cream

Berries:

1. Preheat oven to 350°F.

2. Mix huckleberries with sugar and cornstarch.

3. Transfer berries to 8"x 8" baking pan.

Topping:

1. Mix flour with sugar.

2. Cut butter into small pieces and mix into flour mixture.

3. Slowly add whipping cream to flour mixture.

4. Spread topping evenly over huckleberries.

5. Bake for 50 minutes or until golden.

6. Serve warm topped with vanilla ice cream.

*Slump may be made with 4 cups blueberries if huckleberries are not available.

Recipe adapted for home use by Anthony's Food Consultant, Sharon Kramis, noted Northwest cookbook author whose works include "Berries: A Country Garden Cookbook".

"…I enjoy the daily excitement of knowing I can facilitate growth and productivity of every aspect of Anthony's."
Jeff Arnot, Chief Operating Officer

HALIBUT CAKES

Anthony's at Squalicum Harbor is located just off the I-5 corridor on Squalicum Harbor in Bellwether on the Bay and offers spectacular views of the San Juan Islands and an impressive view of the sunset year round. Anthony's at Squalicum Harbor is also located near Zuanich Park, a bay side park situated among many pleasure yachts and fishing vessels.

Ingredients:

1 lb halibut filet
1¼ cup mayonnaise
¼ cup red bell pepper, diced in ⅛" pieces
¼ tsp kosher salt
2 tbsp dry bread crumbs
2 tbsp chopped fresh parsley
1 tbsp fresh lemon juice
2½ cups panko bread crumbs

1. Cut halibut into 1-2" chunks and steam for four minutes or until cooked through.

2. Cool halibut completely.

3. Mix together: mayonnaise, red pepper, kosher salt, bread crumbs, chopped parsley and lemon juice.

4. Stir in chilled halibut and mix flaking halibut into small pieces.

5. Divide mixture into 8-10 equal round balls.

6. Make balls into patties ¾" thick and coat with panko crumbs.

7. Refrigerate – may be held up to 24 hours.

To Cook:

1. Heat large skillet with clarified butter or salad oil, enough to cover the bottom of the pan.

2. Add cakes and sear until golden on each side, turning only once.

3. After searing, continue to cook on low heat or transfer to baking pan.

4. Place in 350°F oven and heat cakes until they reach 165°F internally.

5. Place two cakes per plate, per person and serve with roasted pepper aioli.

Halibut cakes are very versatile and may be served with a variety of sauces including buerre blanc, roasted red pepper aioli or tartar sauce

"....it is possible to exaggerate and to be duped by gastronomic nincompoops who write of gourmets with a sense of taste so refined that they can tell whether a fish was caught under or between the bridges, and distinguish by its superior flavor the thigh on which the partridge leans while asleep."
Angelo Pellegrini, 'The Unprejudiced Palate' (1948)

REAL ALE

BEER:
So much more
than just a
Breakfast Drink.

AHI TUNA SPINACH SALAD WITH SMOKED BACON VINAIGRETTE

1½ cup baby spinach, destemmed
¼ cup shredded red cabbage
½ Fuji apple
2 oz Brie cheese, sliced
¼ cup toasted almonds
2 Ahi tuna steaks
¼ cup white sesame seeds
Salt and pepper to taste
Sesame oil

Dressing:
1 slice of ¼" applewood smoked bacon
2 tbsp white wine vinegar
1 tbsp pure sesame oil
1 tbsp brown sugar
½ tsp Dijon mustard
¼ tsp diced shallots
Pinch of salt and pepper

1. Lightly rub Ahi steak with sesame oil.

2. Season with salt and pepper to taste and encrust with sesame seeds.

3. Heat olive oil in pan until almost smoking.

4. Sear Ahi about 20-30 seconds each side.

5. Remove from heat and slice into ¼" strips.

6. In the same pan cook bacon until crisp. Add the remaining dressing ingredients and heat for 30-60 seconds.

7. Pour dressing over salad ingredients in a bowl and toss.

8. Serve seared Ahi over salad. Garnish with matchstick apple slices.

Signature Tastes of BELLINGHAM

ARCHER ALE HOUSE
1212 10TH STREET

"…When all is said, its atmosphere (England's pubs) still contains fewer germs of aggression and brutality per cubic foot … than in any other country in which I have lived"
Arthur Koestler, British novelist, journalist, and critic

MORNING GLORY MUFFINS GLUTEN-FREE

2 cups flour
1¼ cups sugar
2 tsp baking soda
2 tsp sugar
½ tsp salt
2 cups coarsely grated carrots
½ cup raisins
½ cup pecans
½ cup shredded coconut, packed
1 large tart apple, peeled and grated
3 eggs
1 cup canola oil
1 tsp vanilla

This recipe can be made gluten free by substituting Bob's Baking Mix for the flour and adding a teaspoon of xanthan gum for leavening.

1. Put dry ingredients into large mixing bowl.

2. Add wet ingredients and mix until blended.

3. Add carrots, raisins, pecans, coconut and apple. Mix well.

4. Fill muffin liners to ¾ full.

5. Put dry ingredients into large mixing bowl.

2. Add wet ingredients and mix until blended.

3. Bake at 375°F for 40-45 minutes or until muffin springs back to touch or a toothpick inserted into the middle comes out clean.

AVELLINO
1329 RAILROAD AVENUE

"...Stella is an Italian beauty. She's in her 30's, from San Francisco and later made her way north. She finally settled here at Avellino. My staff knows that she will pour a consistent shot of espresso every time because she was built to do just that. Come in and see her in action..."
Pat Blakesless, Owner

TOMATO DILL SOUP

Welcome to Avenue Bread where eating well includes delicious choices, such as artisan breads, melt-in-your-mouth pastries, fresh sandwiches to sustain you, and soups and salads to satisfy. We purchase our healthy sprouts from Happy Valley. Our organic mixed greens and soup ingredients come to us, seasonally, from Double Rainbow Farms. Our crisp pickles and sauerkraut come from Pleasant Valley Farms in the Skagit Valley. Our tasty Whatcom County hazelnuts come from Holmquist Hazelnut Farm. Currently we buy our freshly milled flour from Fairhaven Flour Mill.

This recipe is an adaptation of our popular daily soup. For several reasons, the quantities are kept rather vague, but this also provides cooks a chance to find what they like best!

2 small cans of crushed tomatoes (approx 15 oz ea) (or about one quart of fresh crushed tomatoes- this is a great use for cuttings from other tomato projects (salsa, etc.))
1 can (approx 8-12 oz) tomato juice
2 cloves of roasted garlic or 2 tsp garlic powder
1 tsp paprika
1 tsp cayenne
1 tbsp dried dill
¼ cup cream cheese
2 tbsp heavy cream

1. Measure out cream cheese and allow to soften.

2. Slowly cook tomatoes and spices together. The sugar content in tomatoes can make them prone to burning, so if you're not wanting to watch this one all the way through (you want to back-burner it while you do other things), then I recommend double boiling and checking your water every so often...

3. Add cream cheese and heavy cream to hot tomato mixture and blend with a hand blender or fork.

4. Add fresh dill and a dollop of sour cream for a nice garnish.

*If you have a blender or food processor, this soup can be made completely cold (for transport, etc), and then heated just before serving.

Try experimenting with other juices (instead of tomato), and with different amounts of cream cheese/cream and spices. Enjoy!

"...Bread is the king of the table and all else is merely the court that surrounds the king. The countries are the soup, the meat, the vegetables, the salad but bread is king."
Louis Bromfield, American novelist (1896-1956)

FROG LEGS WITH REMOULADE

Frog legs are one of the better-known delicacies of French and Cantonese cuisine. They are also eaten in other regions, such as the Caribbean, the region of Alentejo in Portugal, Slovenia, northwest Greece, the Piemonte region in Italy, Spain, and the midwest southern regions of the United States. The most common kinds of frogs eaten are bullfrogs and leopard frogs as these are abundant in most of the country.

10 ea frog legs, 2-3oz each, the larger the better.
1 qt buttermilk
¼ cup salt
⅛ cup pepper

Dredge:
3 cups flour
3 cups cornmeal
1 cup Panko bread crumbs
½ tbsp garlic powder
1 tbsp onion powder
Salt and pepper to taste
Oil for frying

Remoulade:
1 qt mayonnaise
½ cup ketchup
½ cup cucumber relish
¼ cup minced garlic
¼ cup minced parsley
¼ cup minced shallot
1 tsp Worcestershire sauce
¼ cup lemon juice
¼ cup paprika
1 tbsp stone ground mustard
Salt and pepper to taste

1. Mix all remoulade ingredients and refrigerate overnight.

2. Clean frog legs and marinate legs in buttermilk and seasonings, allow to rest overnight or at least 3 hours.

3. Preheat pan with about a half inch of cooking oil, allow to reach roughly 350°F, or the oil can be seen as shimmering. If the oil starts to smoke, reduce heat.

4. Lightly shake legs from marinade and liberally dredge the legs. Shake off excess breading.

5. Gently place the legs in the pan, be careful to avoid splashing. Allow to reach a golden brown and flip and continue on the other side until golden brown. If the legs appear to darken too quickly, lower the stove temp. If the legs appear to darken in between the joints they are overcooking and remove the legs from the pan.

6. Remove from oil and serve with remoulade sauce.

Editor's Note:

As you can imagine, some unusual seafare might be difficult to find, like frog legs! Enter Vis Seafood on James Street.

Vis Seafood is a fourth-generation seafood purveyor. Many of the recipes in this book call for fresh seafood, such as Bayou on Bay's Frog Legs. Vis either has the seafood in house, or can order virtually anything you might need. Just another way to experience the tastes of Bellingham.

BAYOU ON BAY
1300 BAY STREET

"...Creole is New Orleans city food. Communities were created by the people who wanted to stay and not go back to Spain or France. This is best of all food."
Paul Prudhomme, chef and father of Creole cooking

SEAFOOD SAUTÉ

Tucked away on the waterfront of Bellingham Bay, Bayside Café offers a relaxed dining environment with an incredible view of the water and boats. Seafood lovers will devour this simple yet tasty dish designed by Chef Landon Parent. Fancy restaurants aren't the only place to have a incredible seafood dish. With a few ingredients and easy steps, you'll have an exotic dish on your kitchen table in no time.

About 1 lb fresh halibut, cut into smaller pieces
8-10 oz sea scallops
8-10 jumbo prawns
3 tbsp olive oil
6-8 garlic cloves, minced
1 red onion, sliced thin
1 red bell pepper, sliced thin
1 green bell pepper, sliced thin
1 lemon, zest and juice
1 tomato, diced
1 cup white wine
Salt and pepper
½ cup grated parmesan
1 green onion, chopped
2 tbsp whole butter

1. In a large deep sauté pan heat the olive oil on medium heat until hot. Add your halibut and scallops.

2. Let cook for a few minutes, you're trying to develop a light brown sear on the seafood.

3. Add prawns, then add peppers, onions, garlic.

4. Deglaze with white wine. Add zest and juice of lemon.

5. Season with salt and pepper to taste. Cover with lid and cook 10 minutes.

6. Add diced tomato, parmesan cheese, and butter.

7. Cover and cook until seafood is just done, about 5-8 minutes. Serve in bowls and garnish with parmesan and green onion.

Wine Suggestion:

Sauvignon Blanc

"...Rien ne serait plus fatiguant que mangeant et buvant si Dieu ne leur avait pas fait un plaisir aussi bien qu'une nécessité."
(Nothing would be more tiresome than eating and drinking if God had not made them a pleasure as well as a necessity.)
Voltaire

DEEP FRIED PICKLES

If you like good beer and good conversation, then the Beaver Inn is the place for you. Locals frequent the Beaver knowing that while there is always a place to sit, it never feels empty. While they are famous for their fried chicken, you just might make a few extra friends with an order of the deep fried pickle spears.

24 dill pickle spears, chilled
canola oil for frying

Egg Wash:
2 cups milk
2 eggs
Pinch lemon pepper
Pinch dill weed
Pickle juice

Breading:
2 ½ cups cornmeal
1½ cups all-purpose flour
½ cup lemon pepper
½ cup dill weed
4 tsp paprika
2 tsp garlic salt
Pinch cayenne pepper, or
more to taste

Ranch Dressing:
½ cup buttermilk
½ cup sour cream
3 tbsp minced parsley leaves
2 tbsp chopped green onion
1½ tbsp apple cider vinegar
2 tsp freshly ground pepper
1 tsp Dijon mustard
½ garlic clove, minced
Mayonnaise

1. Using only very cold dill pickle spears, dip pickle into egg wash and then coat with breading. Repeat until no pickles remain.

2. Arrange dipped pickles on a sheet pan lined with waxed paper. Chill for at least 30 minutes.

3. In a deep fryer, heat oil to 375°F (Alternatively, heat oil in a large, heavy pot suitable for deep-frying). Carefully add chilled pickle spears, in batches, to the hot oil and fry for about 3½ minutes or until golden. Remove to a paper towel-lined plate to drain.

Serve with Ranch Dressing.

Egg Wash:

1. In a baking dish, whisk all ingredients together, except pickle juice. Add pickle juice, to taste, and whisk to combine.

Breading:

1. Combine all ingredients in a baking dish.

Ranch Dressing:

1. In a large mixing bowl, stir all ingredients together, except mayonnaise.

2. Add mayonnaise, as needed, to thicken.

3. Refrigerate until ready to serve.

"...Part of the secret of success in life is to eat what you like and let the food fight it out inside."
Mark Twain

From Dave: **5-Alarm Chili**...*Warning: This chili lives up to it's name! If you like your chili flavorful but not hot, simply omit the cayenne pepper. Cascade Radio Group has an annual Chili cook-off that I've only entered once. Others claimed I had burned off their taste buds. I say Yum.*

From Shari:: **Death Weenies**
This is a recipe from my very Southern Grandma Ruby...although there are many different versions out there.

Dave's 5-Alarm Chili
Ingredients:
4 slices bacon, chopped
2 onions, chopped
8 cloves garlic, chopped
2 tsp dried oregano
1 tsp cayenne pepper… if you dare!
3 tbsp paprika
⅛ cup chili powder
1 tsp cumin
4 pounds boneless beef chuck, cut into 1/2-inch cubes
4¾ cups water
1 (12 fluid ounce) can of beer
4 canned chipotle peppers in adobo sauce, seeded and minced
2 tbsp cornmeal

Directions:
1. In a heavy pot, cook the bacon pieces over medium heat until crispy, stirring occasionally. Drain most of the grease, but enough to coat the bottom of the pan.
2. Add the onions and garlic. Cook and stir until the onions are tender. Season with oregano, cayenne pepper, paprika, chili powder and cumin. Cook and stir for about 30 seconds to toast the spices.
3. Stir in the beef, beer, water, chipotle peppers, and cornmeal and bring to a boil. Reduce heat to low. Simmer, uncovered, until beef is tender, 2½ to 3 hours.

Shari's Death Weenies
Ingredients:
1 pkg small cocktail wieners, (I use Little Smokies)
1 lb bacon (I use the center cut....a little less grease and fat)
¾ cup brown sugar

Directions:
1. Cut bacon in half (or thirds).
2. Wrap around smokies.
3. Secure with toothpick and place on old cookie sheet.
4. Sprinkle liberally with brown sugar.
5. Bake at 350° F for 20-30 minutes, until bacon is crispy and brown sugar has caramelized.

These are really messy and will destroy your good cookie sheets so use the old ones your kids have already destroyed!

A Look in the Cupboard of...

Signature Taste of BELLINGHAM

RASPBERRY SALAD

Executive Chef Michael Hannah and his staff at the Bellingham Golf and Country Club pride themselves on the quality and consistency of their menu. The secret to their success? They don't take shortcuts! As a member of Sustainable Connections, they use local Washington purveyors for the freshest ingredients whenever possible. All meats and fish are fresh and cut on premises. The sauces and accompaniments are made in-house using classical techniques.

Dressing (see instructions)
baby field green mix
Sugar-roasted almonds
Butter
Cinnamon
Sugar
Mascarpone or chevre cheese
Lemon zest
Fresh raspberries

Dressing:
2 cups strawberries
6 oz blended olive oil
¼ cup balsamic vinegar
¼ cup red wine vinegar

1. To make sugar roasted almonds, toss whole almonds in melted butter. Season with pinch of cinnamon, and sugar. Toast in 350°F oven until browned, approximately 10 minutes.

2. Lightly toss greens with dressing (less is more). Place in bowl and garnish with almonds, lemon zest and cheese.

Note if using mascarpone cheese, cover a plate with plastic wrap, spread the cheese over wrap using a spatula to less than ¼" thickness and freeze. At plating time, break off pieces of the cheese over the salad. This is a lot easier than trying to get the soft cheese to come off of a spoon.

Dressing:

1. Puree fruit in blender.

2. Add remaining ingredients and puree.

Signature Tastes of BELLINGHAM

BELLINGHAM GOLF & COUNTRY CLUB
3729 MERIDIAN STREET

"...We should look for someone to eat and drink with before looking for something to eat and drink..."
Epicurus

PAN-FRIED HALIBUT WITH PUTTANESCA SAUCE

Delve into fresh Pacific seafood with attitude. The Big Fat Fish Company boldly creates stylistic sushi, fantastic fishfare and a myriad of offerings to astound the most discerning individual. Located a stone's throw from the fishing docks at Fairhaven, Executive Chef Craig Kline draws on the fresh, local fish for inspiration and to highlight a range of subtle and bold tastes.

Puttanesca Sauce:
2 tbsp olive oil
1 clove garlic, mashed
1 tsp anchovy paste
⅛ tsp red pepper flakes
1 tbsp tomato paste
¼ cup white wine
2 tsp capers, drained
4 tomatoes, peeled and diced
2 tbsp black olives, chopped
Salt and pepper, to taste
Juice of ½ lemon
2 tbsp parsley, chopped

Halibut:
4 halibut fillets, 4-5 oz each
Salt and white pepper, to taste
½ cup flour
2 eggs, lightly beaten
2 cups breadcrumbs
1 cup almonds, finely chopped
3 tbsp butter

Halibut:

1. Preheat oven to 350°F.

2. Season halibut with salt and pepper.

3. Place flour in a small bowl. In another bowl, place lightly beaten eggs. In a third bowl place breadcrumbs and almonds.

4. Dredge fish with flour, dip in eggs, then in breadcrumbs and almonds.

5. Heat a large sauté pan over medium heat. Melt butter and fry halibut until golden brown.

6. Transfer to cookie sheet; finish in oven if necessary.

Puttanesca Sauce:

1. In a large sauté pan on medium high, heat oil.

2. Add garlic, anchovy paste, and red pepper flakes and sauté briefly.

3. Add tomato paste and cook for a couple of minutes to get rid of the raw tomato flavor.

4. Reduce heat to low, add white wine and reduce mixture by half.

5. Add capers, tomatoes, and olives. Reduce slightly.

6. Season with salt, pepper, and lemon juice. Sprinkle parsley in right before serving.

THE BIG FAT FISH CO.
1304 12TH STREET

"...Fishermen know that the sea is dangerous and the storm terrible, but they have never found these dangers sufficient reason for remaining ashore..."
Vincent Van Gogh,
requoted by Craig Kline, Executive Chef

AEBLESKIVERS

While the word can be difficult to pronouce (it's actually a Danish word for "sliced apple"-a traditional dessert in Denmark), visitors need only say "...those hollow round pancakes...". Tranplants from Portland, The Bistro is a recent addition to the Bellingham menagerie of culinary delights and is already making an impact with creative offerings and massive portions. Topped off with a siganture Bloody Mary, how do you say "Bellingham's best breakfast" in Danish, anyway?

4 eggs separated
2 tbsp olive oil
2 cups buttermilk

2 cups flour
1 tsp baking powder
1 tsp baking soda
2 tbsp sugar
½ tsp salt

Whipped cream and Maple syrup as needed

1. Combine dry ingredients in bowl of mixer.

2. Whip egg whites to stiff peaks, set aside.

3. Combine egg yolks, buttermilk and olive oil, with mixer running add to flour mixture.

4. Fold in the egg whites, and adjust consistency as needed.

5. Sprayed with canola oil, an Aebleskiver Pan which should be heated up medium- high on the stove, pour batter into each cup 3/4 to the rim.

6. When the batter begins to bubble, rotate the Aebleskivers using a skewer or toothpick. The batter should slide deeper into the cup and continue cooking. Continue this step every 30 seconds until a full sphere is made by the batter.

7. Continue to rotate the Aebleskivers to allow heat to cook the inside and avoid burning the outside.

8. Once plated, top with candied bacon, pecans, maple creme fraiche (substitute whipped cream if needed), and powered sugar. Serve with maple syrup.

THE BISTRO ON MAGNOLIA STREET
113 EAST MAGNOLIA STREET

"God gives all birds their food but does not drop it into their nests..."
Danish proverb

SPANISH GARLIC PRAWNS

Signature Tastes of BELLINGHAM

It all started with one man...and a flaming grill...Executive Chef Jack Niemann. Born in Germany in 1938, he immigrated to Canada in 1955. In 1960, he opened his first self-owned restaurant, tripled the business within 18 months and sold the same for 3 times the purchase price. The first Black Forest was built in 1968, and was called "an oasis in a culinary desert." That legacy of excellence in dining is being continued today under the leadership of Chef David Williams.

¼ cup olive oil
2 tsp chopped garlic
½ tsp crushed red pepper
4 U-15 prawns
Seasoning salt
(garlic, salt and pepper in equal parts)

1. Over low heat, add olive oil, red peppers and garlic.

2. Saute until peppers are almost done (4 minutes).

3. Now add prawns.

4. Saute until prawns are pink on one side then flip, cook, and done! About 1½ minutes each side.

BLACK FOREST STEAKHOUSE
1263 BARKLEY BOULEVARD

"...My Culinary Art is wasted...
on Those who Salt before they have tasted..."
Jack Niemann, founder-Black Forest Steak House

Cuban Pulled Pork (Pan con Lechon)

Nearly as far away as you can get in the lower 48 from Bellingham lives the inspiration for the Book Fare Cafe's Cuban pulled pork. Slow-roasted with lots of garlic and onions, seasoned with a luxurious splash of citrus, this sandwich is a little taste of the tropics in the Pacific Northwest.

1 boneless pork picnic roast (5-6 lbs)
2 large sweet onions, peeled and quartered with the root left intact
4 heads of garlic, cloves separated and peeled
2 bay leaves
1 tbsp whole black peppercorns
coarse sea salt

For the Mojo:
½ c grapeseed oil
½ c fresh squeezed lime juice
1 head garlic, cloves separated, peeled, and sliced (8-10 cloves)
1 medium sweet onion, thinly sliced
1 tsp freshly ground pepper
1 tsp coarse sea salt
3 tbsp cilantro leaves, chopped

1. In a roasting pan, add about a half inch of water and add the onion, garlic, bay leaves and peppercorns.

2. Rest the pork roast atop the onions and season with salt.

3. Cover with parchment paper then foil or a tight fitting lid and roast at 275°F for 4 to 6 hours, until the pork is tender enough to shred with a fork.

4. In a large bowl, pull the pork apart with two forks, incorporating the roasted onions, garlic and pan jus. Set aside while you prepare the mojo.

5. Add the garlic, onions, pepper and salt to the lime juice.

6. Over medium heat in a high sided pan, bring the grapeseed oil to 300°F.

7. Add the lime juice mixture to the hot oil and immediately cover and remove from heat. This will splatter, so it's important to use a pan with high sides and a tight fitting lid.

8. Add the cilantro leaves to the mojo and pour over the pulled pork.

Cuban bread is a soft, dense white bread, but we've found Avenue Bread's Ciabogies to be the perfect vehicle for this Pan con Lechon.

Book Fair

3RD FLOOR, 1200 11TH STREET

"...I'm going to break one of the rules of the trade here. I'm going to tell you some of the secrets of improvisation. Just remember—it's always a good idea to follow the directions exactly the first time you try a recipe. But from then on, you're on your own." ..."
James Beard

BOOMER BURGER
AND HARD ICE CREAM SHAKE

World Famous Waffle Fries.
Hard Ice Cream Milkshakes.
Car Hop Service.
How do we describe these "Signature" recipes?
We don't. We let Chris Irwin, owner, do it in his words...

BURGERS

Boomers Drive-In Recipe #0101

The Boomer Burger

- Toasted Sesame Seed Bun Baked Fresh Daily
- American Cheese
- **Large, Juicy Beef Patty** (No tiny fast food soy burgers)
- Pickles, Onions on request — No Charge
- Freshly Cut Iceberg Lettuce and Two Thick Slices of Ripe Tomato
- Secret Sauce (Ingredients: Mayo, Ketchup, Garlic — Sorry, the rest is classified info.)

Special Instructions to the Cook:
1. Cook to order (Do not let it sit under the heat lamps like the other guys).
2. Honor all special customer requests — extra tomato, extra onion, extra pickle, etc.
3. Handle burger with special care.

Boomers DRIVE-IN

310 North Samish Way ◆ Open 7 Days/Week ◆ 647-BOOM

A Glimpse of Boomers Recipe Cards

TREATS

Boomers Drive-In Recipe #0201

The Hard Ice Cream Shake

Old fashioned method of preparation only!

1. Add 3 large scoops of quality hard ice cream.
2. **Add one or more of the following:** Fresh Bananas, Strawberries, Black Berries, Mocha, Vanilla, Pineapple, Cherry, Peanut Butter, Orange, Chocolate Chip Mint, or the Special Flavor of the Week.
3. Add 3 oz milk and blend for 3-4 minutes until the shake has reached the ultimate shake lovers consistency — thick yet viscous enough to flow through a 3/8" wide straw.

Special Instructions to the Car-Hop:
Never use the high-tech shake machines — these machines use a low-cost product called "shake-mix" that freezes and mixes air into the mix, producing a much-too-sweet imitation air-filled shake. *Yuck!*

Boomers DRIVE-IN

310 North Samish Way ◆ Open 7 Days/Week ◆ 647-BOOM

"...You can find your way across this country using burger joints the way a navigator uses stars....We have munched Bridge burgers in the shadow of the Brooklyn Bridge and Cable burgers hard by the Golden Gate, Dixie burgers in the sunny South and Yankee Doodle burgers in the North....We had a Capitol Burger -- guess where. And so help us, in the inner courtyard of the Pentagon, a Penta burger."

Charles Kuralt, journalist. (1934–1997)

Yam Alechiladas

The Boundary Bay Brewery & Bistro caters to locals and out-of-towners alike with their unique atmosphere of energy, artistry, community and hospitality. While their beer has won award after award, it is balanced by a selection of food that will bring you back all on its own. Boundary Bay chefs and brewmasters push the envelope to make a very big and flavorful impact on your taste buds. Like a new kind of music, it may take a few samplings to build your palette but soon you will be coming back for more.

Signature Tastes of **BELLINGHAM**

2½ lbs cooked, peeled yams
4 tbsp roasted garlic
½ cup caramelized onions
1 tsp ground coriander
1½ tsp dried thyme
1½ tsp kosher salt
1 tsp white pepper
¼ tsp cayenne
2 oz shredded cheddar cheese
2 oz shredded Monterey Jack

Mole:
2 anaheim peppers
1 jalapeno pepper
2 poblano peppers
1 red bell pepper
1 roma tomato
1 yellow onion
1 tbsp chopped garlic
1 dried chipotle
1 ancho pepper
1 tsp red pepper flakes
1 tbsp sesame seeds
¾ tsp ground cumin
¾ tsp dried thyme
2 cups vegetable stock
½ bunch cilantro
(2) 6" white corn tortillas
6 oz unsweetened chocolate

Mole:

1. Seed and rough chop the peppers and tomatoes.

2. Rough chop the onions; tear tortillas into quarters.

3. Put all ingredients except the chocolate into a medium size pot and simmer for an hour.

4. Break the chocolate into pieces and place in a bowl large enough to fit on top of the simmering pot.

5. Place the bowl of chocolate on top of the simmering pot to melt the chocolate.

6. After a half hour drain the liquids from the solids.

7. Puree the solids in a food processor or blender. Add the liquids and the melted chocolate.

Filling:

1. Puree the roasted garlic and caramelized onions in a food processor or blender.

2. Mash the yams in a large bowl. Add shredded cheese.

3. Add the processed ingredients and spices to the mashed yams to thoroughly combine all ingredients.

Enchiladas:

1. Fill tortillas, roll and place in an oven-proof pan. Bake at 325 °F for 25 minutes.

2. Top with Mole and serve.

BOUNDARY BAY BREWERY
1107 RAILROAD AVENUE

"...Without question, the greatest invention in the history of mankind is beer. Oh, I grant you that the wheel was also a fine invention, but the wheel does not go nearly as well with pizza."
Dave Berry

Cedar Planked Salmon with Peach Barbeque Sauce

Step into Café Culinaire, Bellingham Technical College's fully operational restaurant, located on the BTC campus, in G building, where BTC's Culinary Arts program students exclusively prepare all dishes under the supervision of our chef instructors. They utilize their knowledge at each station of a busy kitchen and participate in managing all levels of restaurant operations.

¼ cup unsalted butter
½ red onion, minced
2 cloves garlic, minced
¼ cup soy sauce
½ tbsp Dijon mustard
¼ cup packed brown sugar
¼ cup fresh lemon juice
½ cup peach preserves
¼ cup red wine vinegar
5 lbs boneless salmon fillet;
cut into 5 oz portions
¼ cup fresh chives, snipped
Cedar shingles

1. Combine all the ingredients for the barbecue sauce in a large sauce pan.

2. Bring to boil; reduce the heat and simmer for ½ hour, or until slightly thicken.

3. Set aside half the sauce for serving.

4. Place salmon fillets on cedar shingles.

5. Baste with ½ of the barbecue sauce and bake at 350°F until firm to touch about 10-15 minutes.

6. Serve with additional heated BBQ sauce over salmon, sprinkle with chives.

3028 LINDBERGH AVENUE, BUILDING G

CAFÉ CULINAIRE

"...Gastronomy has been the joy of all peoples through the ages. It produces beauty and wit and goes hand in hand with goodness of heart and a consideration of others."
Charles Pierre Monselet (1825-88) French journalist and author

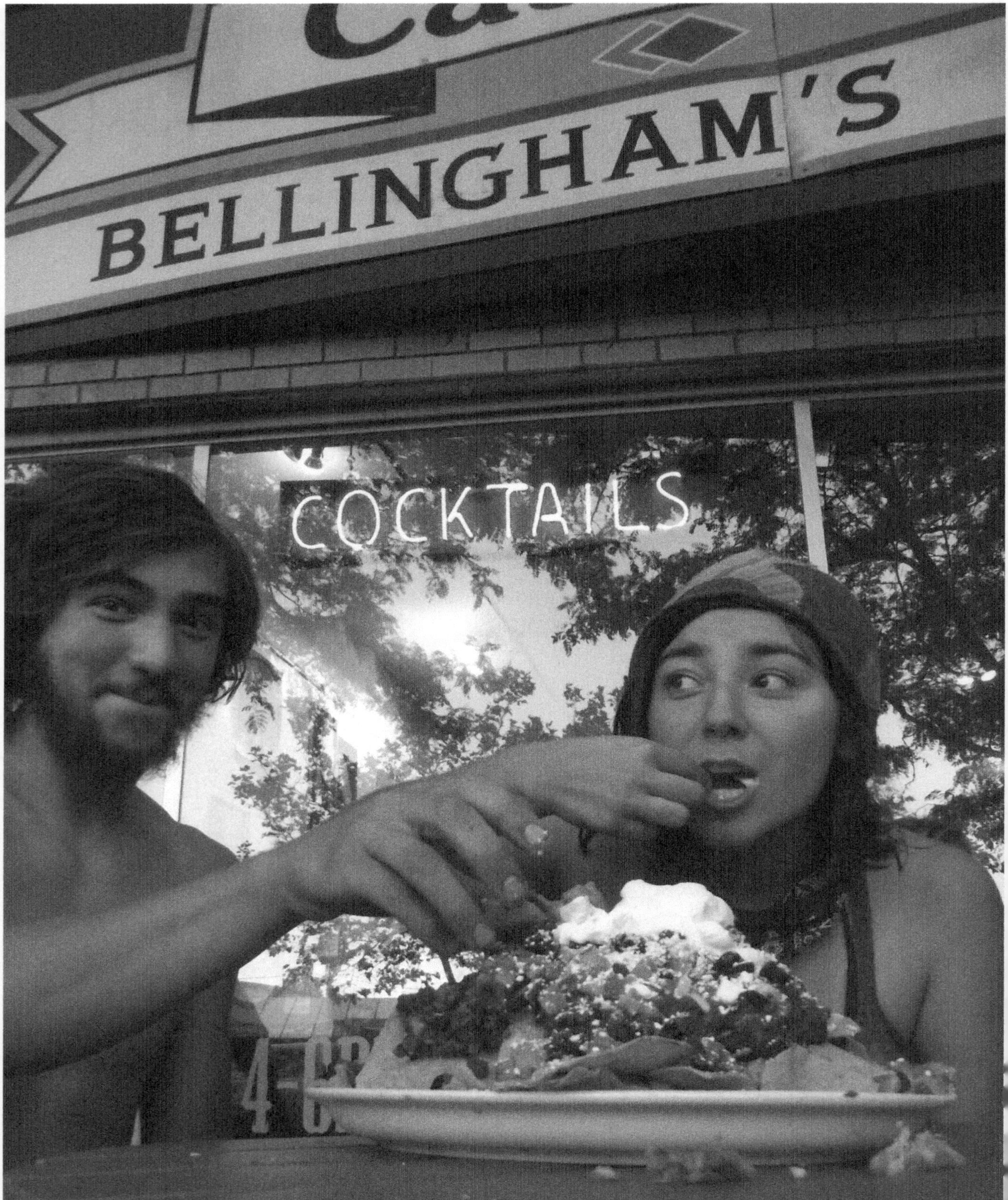
BELLINGHAM'S
COCKTAILS

CHIPOTLE SMOTHER

The word burrito means "little donkey" in Spanish, coming from burro, which means "donkey". The name burrito possibly derives from the appearance of a rolled-up wheat tortilla, which vaguely resembles the ear of its namesake animal, or from bedrolls and packs that donkeys carried. Mexican popular tradition tells the story of a man named Juan Mendez who used to sell tacos at a street stand, using a donkey as a transport for himself and the food. To keep the food warm, Juan wrapped the food in a large flour tortilla inside individual napkins. Hence the burrito was born.

2 yellow onions
5 Roma tomatoes
2 serrano peppers, deseeded
¾ cup butter, unsalted
⅛ cup olive oil
3 cloves garlic
⅛ cup roasted garlic soup base
2 cups water
32 oz size can diced tomatoes
8 oz can chipotles in adobo sauce
2 tsp dried oregano
1 tsp dried basil
1 to 2 bunches cilantro
1 tsp thyme
1 tsp crushed red pepper
1 tsp onion powder

1. On a cookie sheet drizzle olive oil on halved roma tomatoes and one of the onions cut in half and peeled. Salt and pepper to taste. Roast for 20-30 minutes in oven at high heat until edges are browned/blackened.

2. While vegetables are roasting, in a large pot melt butter and olive oil on med-low heat. Add second chopped onions and chopped garlic and cook until softened, about 10 minutes.

3. Dissolve soup base in water, pour into pot along with all ingredients and bring to a boil, adding roasted vegetables as soon as they are done. Lower heat and simmer for 20-30 minutes.

4. Using a hand held food processor wand or large blender, pull pot off heat and blend simmered mixture until smooth, adding salt and pepper to taste.

Serve on any burrito of your choice. We suggest a burrito made with a garlic-herb tortilla, whole black beans mildly spiced with cumin and salt, Monterey Jack cheese, diced onion, sour cream and spinach leaves.

CASA QUE PASA
1415 RAILROAD AVENUE

"…I was eating burritos with this girl and she asked me to be her prom date. How could I say no? We went and had a great time."
Josh Hartnett

Dark Chocolate Dessert Topping

Chocolate Necessities has been importing the finest Callebaut Chocolates for use in our gourmet truffles and solid chocolates since 1987. We believe you won't find a smoother, creamier milk chocolate or richer, more layered dark anywhere. The choice to use Callebaut chocolate is the result of years of careful comparison of the world's finest chocolates.

12 oz bag Colombian 65% chocolate chips

1 ½ cups whipping cream

1. Begin warming chocolate in a double boiler at medium heat, stirring often until all chunks are melted.

2. Decrease heat to medium low.

3. In a separate saucepan, heat cream on high until a skin begins to form on top. Do not boil.

4. Pour the hot cream into the chocolate and whisk, beginning in the center and moving outward until the cream and chocolate are completely mixed and the mixture becomes silky and thick.

5. Serve right away over vanilla bean ice cream or Chocolate Necessities vanilla gelato.

"... the taste of chocolate is a sensual pleasure in itself, existing in the same world as sex... For myself, I can enjoy the wicked pleasure of chocolate... entirely by myself. Furtiveness makes it better..."
Dr. Ruth Westheimer

SHELLFISH BOWL

A brewery and restaurant offering consistent, unique, quality-driven craft beers and beverages with creative, locally-influenced fresh American cuisine in Old Town, Bellingham. The owners Mari and Will Kemper have brought quality craft beers to their customers across America, Mexico and Turkey since 1984 and are glad to bring guests their exceptional beer and food in an inspiring, friendly and lively environment.

1 stalk celery, chopped fine
1 onion, chopped fine
1 tomato, chopped small
2 cloves minced garlic
¼ tsp fennel seed
¼ tsp Herbes de Provence
¼ tsp red chili flakes
3 tbsp of olive oil
4 cups cleaned shellfish such as clams, mussels, or combination
¼ cup Chuckanut Brewery Kolsch

1. In a heavy saucepan sauté celery, tomato, onion, garlic, herbes & spices on medium to low heat.

2. Cook until soft.

3. Bring to a simmer

4. When bubbling add ¼ cup Chuckanut Brewery Kolsch (or any fruity beer), red chili flakes, and shellfish.

5. Simmer uncovered until shells open.

6. Discard any unopened shellfish.

7. Divide into 4 separate serving bowls and serve with toast or French bread.

CHUCKANUT BREWERY
601 WEST HOLLY STREET

"...' It's no fish ye're buyin, its men's lives.' by Sir Walter Scott...That's why we try to use the best local ingredients on our menu to go with our great, local, and fresh beers..."
Mari Kemper, Co-owner

*This is a bread recipe for **Multigrain Rolls** that takes less than two hours from start to finish. The molasses and the rye give it a nice earthy flavor. The rolls can be used for sandwiches, but I usually eat them for breakfast, topped with jam or honey after they have been split and toasted on a cast iron griddle. (They always get stuck in the toaster...)*

1⅔ cups lukewarm water
¾ tsp salt
3 tbsp blackstrap molasses
3 tbsp vegetable oil
1 cup white bread flour
2 cups whole wheat bread flour
½ cup uncooked oatmeal
½ cup dark rye flour
⅓ cup wheat bran
⅓ cup wheat germ
2 tbsp wheat gluten
3 tsp dry yeast

1. Combine water, salt, molasses and oil in mixing bowl or bread machine. (I use a machine.)

2. Add flour and other dry ingredients to bread machine- or in a bowl, mix gradually, stirring and then kneading about 20 minutes.

3. Let rise in a warm place 20 minutes and knead for another 10 minutes or so, adding more flour if it seems too soft and sticky.

4. Then, form dough into a log about 12 inches long, and cut log into about 10 slices. (They don't have to be the same size; I like some big meal-sized ones and smaller ones for bedtime snacks.)

5. Put these slices on a greased cooking sheet (I use a pizza pan) leaving some space for them to spread out as they rise, and put them in a slightly warm oven for 15 or 20 minutes. They should almost double in volume.

6. Then, remove from oven, preheat to 375°F, and bake for 28 minutes.

7. Allow to cool for 10 minutes, and enjoy!

A Look in the Cupboard of...

Signature Tastes of BELLINGHAM

WHISKY CRAB SOUP

Nestled in a nondescript building on the cliff edge off North State Street, this is by far the most requested recipe for the Cliff House. Taking time to do it right is the key. Now, enjoying a cup of this overlooking Bellingham Bay, sipping on one of the restaurant's outstanding wine offerings, its easy to understand why good things take time.

Red Sauce:
1 cup olive oil
6 cups shredded carrots
3 cups chopped red onion
2 tbsp dried basil
¼ cup chopped garlic
1 #10 can diced tomatoes

Soup Base:
3 cups flour
1 lb butter
¼ cup chicken base
¼ cup fish base
1½ gallons water

Soup Ingredients:
3 ½ cups Red Sauce
2 tbsp Old Bay Seasoning
1 tbsp white pepper
1 cup lemon juice
2 tbsp Worcestershire
2 tbsp Tabasco
½ gallon heavy cream
½ cup Sherry
2 oz Jack Daniels
3 cups Dungeness crab meat

Red Sauce:

1. Combine following ingredients in a large stock pot: olive oil, carrots, onions, basil, and garlic.

2. Cook over high heat, stirring regularly, until carrots are tender, then add tomatoes.

3. Return to a boil, then remove from heat and let stand 5 minutes to cool. Puree mixture in blender until smooth.

Soup Base:

1. Bring water to a boil in a large stock pot, and add fish and chicken base.

2. Return to a boil then reduce heat.

3. Melt butter for Roux in a sauce pan over high heat.

4. Add flour slowly to boiling butter.

5. Remove from heat and stir until smooth.

6. Add Roux to stock, mix well, cover and let cook over low heat 5 minutes.

Soup:

1. Add all but last 4 ingredients to the soup base, and mix well.

2. Add cream, sherry, whisky and crab meat, stirring gently but well.

3. Slowly heat to serve to prevent from scorching.

"...of all the great items that we offer, this recipe has brought more comments and I feel defines our restaurant as much as any other recipe..."
Jon Wilkerson, manager

WAIKIKI PIZZA

All of the pizzas that we serve in our restaurant, including the "Waikiki," feature a deep-dish style crust. For easy breezy home preparation, any store bought pizza crust will work just fine, without sacrificing the flavor of the islands!

8 oz diced chicken breast
⅔ cup sweet BBQ sauce
(1) 14" prebaked pizza dough
10 oz mozzarella cheese
¾ cup diced red onions
½ cup cooked bacon crumbles
¼ cup chopped cilantro

1. Preheat oven to 400°F.

2. Toss diced chicken in 2 tbsp of BBQ sauce.

3. Spread remaining BBQ sauce onto pizza dough.

4. Sprinkle mozzarella cheese in an even layer over BBQ sauce.

5. Top the pizza with the chicken and red onions, followed by bacon.

6. Bake for 13-18 minutes or until the cheese is completely melted and the crust has crisped to your liking.

7. Before serving, garnish with fresh cilantro. If you like a little heat, add red pepper flakes after cilantro.

Enjoy!

"...Ask not what you can do for your country.
Ask what's for lunch..."
Orson Welles

PEANUT BUTTER PIE

"Mama Colophon", the imaginary founder and logo of the Colophon Cafe, came about in 1985, when the cafe opened. Serving only lattes, ice cream and bagels with cream cheese, all containing milk products, the proprietors decided a cow was a likely mascot. After purchasing a cow silk-screen for the wall, the rest was history. Now, cows peer from every wall and post and Colophon Café's desserts have been featured in almost every Northwest publication as well as Bon Appetit and Fodor's Northwest.

Pie Crust:
2 ½ cups chocolate cookie crumbs
¼ cups butter, melted

Pie Filling:
9 oz cream cheese
¾ cup crunchy peanut butter
¾ cup brown sugar
½ tsp vanilla extract
2 cup heavy whipping cream
¼ cup powdered sugar

Ganache:
1 cup semi-sweet chocolate chips
¼ cup half & half

Pie Crust:

1. Combine cookie crumbs and butter well by hand or in food processor.

2. Press crust into 9 inch pie pan, and bake for 7-10 minutes at 350°F.

Pie Filling:

1. Mix cream cheese, peanut butter, brown sugar and vanilla together in a large bowl and set aside.

2. Whip cream on low speed for two minutes.

3. Add powdered sugar and continue to whip on high until peaks form.

4. Fold the whipped cream mixture into the peanut butter mixture to create pie filling.

5. Spoon the pie filling into 9 inch chocolate cookie crust pie pan. Spread filling evenly and freeze for 3 hours.

Ganache

1. Melt chocolate chips and half & half in a separate bowl.

2. Quickly spread ganache evenly over the top of the pie filling. Garnish with 1-2 tbsp of chopped peanuts.

The Pies may be stored in Tupperware in the freezer. To thaw, place on counter for 20-30 minutes before cutting. The pies cut easier when partially frozen.

"...Where your chocolate and peanut butter fantasy comes true. One of our most requested decadent desserts is a local favorite...."
David Killian, Owner

Ossian Williams and his mother
Stephanie enjoying a sweet treat at
the Co-op.

WILD RICE AND KALE SALAD

Our Wild Rice and Kale Salad is one of our most popular and delicious deli salads in the Swan Café – it is a light (yet hearty!) salad with a subtle lemon dressing that is packed with nutrition and great flavor! You can find many more popular recipes on our website at www.communityfood.coop and on our blog at www.communityfoodcoop.wordpress.com.

Salad:
1 cup wild rice
8 cups kale, shredded
½ cup red bell pepper, diced
½ cup green onion, chopped
3 cups boiling water
Salt to taste

Dressing:
3 tbsp lemon juice
3 tbsp extra-virgin olive oil
2 tsp sea salt
1 tsp black pepper

Salad:

1. Rinse rice well.

2. Add to 3 cups boiling water, salted to taste, in a heavy stock pot.

3. Return to a boil.

4. Reduce heat and simmer (covered) for 50 – 60 minutes or just until kernels puff open.

5. Uncover and fluff with a fork.

6. Simmer for five additional minutes, and then drain any remaining water. Set aside to cool.

7. Whisk together dressing ingredients.

8. Toss cooled rice with the dressing until coated and loose.

9. Add shredded kale and toss.

10. Add remaining ingredients and toss.

COMMUNITY FOOD CO-OP/SWAN CAFÉ
1220 NORTH FOREST STREET AND 315 WESTERLY ROAD

"...Food may be our middle name, but it all starts with Community!"
Motto of Community Food Co-op

CORN DOG LOLLIPOPS

Now, no doubt the idea of thirty-two one-ounce Corn Dog Lollipops is intimidating; but rest assured, thirty-one won't be enough. And you don't have to eat them all by yourself, you can have a friend over, maybe someone you haven't seen in awhile. Maybe you should call that person you have been thinking about lately, that person you've been meaning to call for weeks. They've been thinking about you too. Anyway, here is the recipe.

Lollies:
2 lbs ground pork (70/30)
1¾ tbsp salt
1¾ tbsp white sugar
2 tsp sage
2 tsp black pepper
¼ tsp dry mustard
¼ tsp paprika
⅛ tsp celery seed
⅛ tsp mace
A pinch of lemon zest

Batter:
1 cup flour
⅔ cup yellow corn meal
¼ cup white sugar
1½ tsp baking powder
1 tsp salt
2 tbsp melted butter
1 egg, beaten
½ tsp baking soda
1¼ cups of buttermilk

1. First step, put on your favorite Underground Kingz album.

2. Second step, gather your ingredients. You're really making two things here, the lollies and the batter.

3. Third step, preheat your oven to 375°F.

4. Step number 4: Set your fryer at 325°F or bring a pot of vegetable oil up to the same temperature on the stove top. You need enough oil so that the lollipops will be fully submerged, say two inches. Hot oil (like the Wu-Tang) is nothing you wanna mess around with, treat it with respect.

5. Fifth Step, thoroughly mix your ground pork and seasonings. Mold your lollies. Each one should be about 1 ounce. Place them on a greased cookie sheet and in the 375°F oven for around 15 minutes or until the pork reaches 145-150°F. This can be done up to two days in advance.

6. Numero seis, make your batter by thoroughly mixing all the ingredients together.

7. Step seven is where everything gets exciting. Skewer the sausage balls. Toothpicks should suffice, but you might want to use something a little bigger. Did I mention oil can be hot? Dip the sausage balls in corn batter and place them in the hot oil. Fry until golden brown, it won't take long. Then, remove from the hot oil and place on a paper towel to absorb excess grease.

8. Step Eight: Mouth full of delicious pork and lips covered in crumbs and grease, turn to the person sitting on the bear skin rug next to you. Look them in the eyes. Hold that look till it starts to make them a little uncomfortable. Now, finally, you can tell them everything you've ever needed to.

COPPER HOG
1327 NORTH STATE STREET

"You can catch us on the late | Roll' dice blowin' and sippin' on the bar straight | We got the red drink orange drink purple drink | Laughin' at these mark $@#s that say | They never heard of drink | Half gallon big gulp | Big red big cup | drink mixed up | Blowin' sweets and lightin' cigs up"
Bun B of UGK

TAPENADE CROSTINI

D'Anna's started in the early 90's with a wholesale pasta business in Seattle. Other restaurants were getting such rave reviews from the pastas, they decided to open their own café in Bellingham. With fresh handmade pasta, gnocchi, ravioli, home-made bread and many other favorites prepared from scratch daily, it's no wonder they had lines out the door within a few months.

¼ cup whole garlic
1½ bunches of parsley
½ cup lemon juice
½ cup capers
1 cup olive oil
½ tbsp black pepper
2 cups nicoise olives
1 can black olives
Crostini

1. Mix garlic, parsley, lemon juice, capers and olive oil together in food processor and transfer to a large bowl.

2. Add black pepper and olives; mix all ingredients together.

3. Toast crostini, spread tapenade on and top with a dollop of sour cream. Garnish with fresh parsley.

D'ANNA'S CAFÉ ITALIANO
1317 NORTH STATE STREET

" ...the simple beauty of Italian cooking is its simplicity...you make beautiful food by using beautiful ingredients."
Mario Batali, chef and restauranteur

FETA, MUSHROOM, TOMATO AND SPINACH SCRAMBLE

American financier and philanthropist "Diamond" Jim Brady was legendary for his collection of diamond jewelry, and for his gargantuan appetite. He was known to eat 6 or 7 giant lobsters, dozens of oysters, clams and crabs, 2 ducks, steak and desserts at a single sitting. He would also mash a pound of caviar into his baked potatoes. George Rector, a New York restaurateur said he was "the best twenty-five customers I ever had." Today, Diamond Jim's Grill continues this homage to large appetites in the Fountain District.

3 XL eggs, whisked
2 oz sliced mushrooms
(White, Brown, etc. - Shiitake is my favorite because of the texture)
2 oz chopped tomato
1 handful fresh spinach leaveo
1 tbsp canola Oil
3 oz cooked chopped sausage if you gotta have meat!

1. Start by sautéing the sliced mushrooms (and the pre-cooked sausage) in the canola oil until tender.

2. Add the whisked eggs and stir as they start to firm up. Before the eggs are set, add the fresh spinach leaves and turn them into the eggs.

3. Continue cooking the eggs, mushrooms and spinach until the eggs are done to your liking.

4. Lastly add the fresh tomato and Feta cheese and turn it into the finished dish.

5. Turn off the heat so the tomatoes stay fresh and the Feta cheese stays intact.

6. Add your favorite seasoning and serve with hash brown potatoes or if at Diamond Jim's Grill, they are served with American Fried Potatoes and a warm homemade biscuit.

DIAMOND JIM'S GRILL
2400 MERIDIAN STREET

"...Brady is described as having routinely begun his day 'with a hefty breakfast of eggs, breads, muffins, grits, pancakes, steaks, chops, fried potatoes, and pitchers of orange juice. He'd stave off mid-morning hunger by downing two or three dozen clams or oysters'..."
John Mariani, America Eats Out

DAN PIKE MAYOR, CITY OF BELLINGHAM

It was first written by Jonathon Swift..."They say fish should swim thrice ... first it should swim in the sea ... then it should swim in butter, and at last, sirrah, it should swim in good claret...". While there is no claret in this, few could argue that the **Halibut with Shallot, Kalamata and Capers Tapenade** *are swimming along just fine.*

(4) 6-ounce halibut fillets
2 tbsp olive oil
2 large shallots, finely chopped
¼ tsp crushed red pepper
½ cup Kalamata olives, pitted and chopped
¼ cup chopped fresh cilantro
1 tbsp drained capers
½ cup lime juice, divided
Salt and pepper to taste

1. Sprinkle fish with salt and pepper.

2. Place fillets on a medium-hot grill, and baste with a little of the lime juice.

3. Turn fish at about 7 minutes, basting the top again with lime juice.

4. After about 5 minutes more, when filets show distinct grill marks on exterior and are flaky and moistly opaque inside, transfer fish to a platter.

5. Heat olive oil in skillet. Add shallots and crushed red pepper; sauté 1 minute.

6. Mix in olives and capers; sauté an additional minute. Remove from heat.

7. Add lime juice and cilantro, and season with salt and pepper.

8. Spoon tapenade over fish.

Signature Tastes of BELLINGHAM

HORCHATA

Horchata is an old-world drink that was enjoyed by the Aztecs. Today this agua fresca is served throughout Mexico. Where did the name "Horchata" came from? Well, there's an old story about a girl who offered some of the drink to the visiting King of Catalunya and Aragon. After enjoying the drink, the king asked, "Que es aixo?" (What is this?). The girl answered, "Es leche de Chufa" (Chufa milk), to which the King replied, "Aixo no es llet, aixo es or, xata!" (This is not milk; this is gold, child). The fame spread throughout the country and the name of the drink started to be known in Spanish as Orchata.

Signature Tastes of **BELLINGHAM**

1 cup uncooked white rice
¼ cup ground, blanched almonds or almond meal
½ tbsp ground cinnamon
6 cups water, divided
½ tsp vanilla extract
½ cup sugar
Cheesecloth

1. Put rice in a blender and grind to a powder about 2-3 minutes. Grind to as smooth as possible. Combine the ground rice , ground almonds and cinnamon.

2. Put mixture into a blender and add 2 cups of water and blend again for 2 minutes.

3. Strain the mixture into pitcher through several layers of dampened cheesecloth. Do not skip this step or the drink will have a chalky taste.

4. Add 4 more cups of water and the vanilla and sugar, stirring until the sugar is dissolved. If the mixture is too thick, add some additional water. Horchata should have the consistency of milk. The drink is supposed to be sweet, so taste and add more or less sugar as desired.

5. Cover and refrigerate. Horchata will keep for several days, refrigerated. Serve it chilled in tall glasses over ice.

"Aixo no es llet, aixo es or, xata!"
(This is not milk; this is gold, child!)
King of Catalunya and Aragon

CIOPPINO

It was developed in the late 1800s by Italian fishermen who settled in the North Beach section of San Francisco. The name comes from ciuppin, a word in the Ligurian dialect of the port city of Genoa, meaning "to chop" or "chopped" which described the process of making the stew by chopping up various leftovers of the day's catch. At least one restaurant in San Francisco, the eponymous Cioppino's, describes an apocryphal story in which the name derived from the heavily Italian-accented cry of the wharf cooks for the fishermen to "chip in" some of their catch to the collective soup pot.

6 clams
6 mussels
½ lobster
2 oz fish stock
2 oz white
1 oz lemon juice
Salt and pepper to taste
1 tsp garlic, minced
2 prawns
3 scallops
3 calamari
¼ lb salmon, cubed
1½ cups marinara sauce
1 oz whipped butter
Parsley
Lemon Wedge
Grilled garlic bread

1. Combine first 8 ingredients (clams through garlic) into a large stock pan and cook over medium heat until the clams open up and the lobster is almost cooked completely.

2. Add remaining ingredients to the pot and cook covered until shrimp just turn pink (about 2-3 minutes).

3. Add the whipped butter last, and toss to mix well (sauce will glisten).

4. Put in a pasta bowl and garnish with chopped parsley and a lemon wedge

5. Serve with garlic bread on the side.

"…Dan…[appeared] not possessed of more money than would be required to buy most men a square meal, I know that he was of a saving disposition and always had considerable sums of money."
A. G. Robinson, pioneer of San Juan County and colleague of "Dirty" Dan Harris

HABANERO JELLY

The habanero pepper is 85 centuries old. It is believed to have originated in Cuba. Although it is now grown in Belize, Costa Rica, Texas, and even California, the majority of habanero peppers are harvested by the ton in the Yucatan each year. The habanero pepper is definitely one of the hottest peppers known to man at 200,000 - 300,000 Scoville heat units. It is second only to the Red Savina habanero pepper at 350,000 - 550,000 Scoville heat units. To put this in perspective, the Tabasco pepper is only at 30,000 - 50,000 Scoville heat units while the jalapeno pepper is rated at a mere 3,500 - 4,000 Scoville heat units! Now that's hot!

5 habanero peppers
4 red bell peppers
1½ cup distilled vinegar
6 ½ cups sugar
(2) 3 oz packets liquid pectin

1. Put on rubber gloves! Like the kind for washing dishes.

2. Remove stems and seeds from habanero peppers.

3. Place in blender and add ½ cup distilled vinegar.

4. Remove stems and seeds from red peppers (save the seeds).

5. Blend habaneros, vinegar, and red peppers until pureed.

6. Pour mixture into the sauce pot on stove.

7. Add: 6½ cups sugar and remaining 1 cup vinegar, seeds (from red bell peppers).

8. Bring mixture to a vigorous boil. Cook for 5 minutes, add (2) 3 oz packets of liquid pectin and boil for 2 additional minutes.

9. Transfer to plastic 4 qt container and refrigerate w/o lid. Stir during cooling to break up clumps on surface.

Yield 2 QTs.   Shelf life 30 days.

"Ten years ago it was very difficult to make people understand. They thought they shouldn't pay more than ten bucks for a Mexican dish because it was just beans, rice and sour cream. Because of Mexican fast food and other places they got used to food that was very poorly prepared. But Mexican cuisine deserves the same care as any other cuisine." Carlos Melendez

DOS PADRES
1111 HARRIS AVENUE

"…Wish I had time for just one more bowl of chili."
The dying words of Kit Carson

BEET CAKE

Founded in 1994 by Erin Baker, Erin Baker's Wholesome Baked Goods continues to thrive as a woman owned and operated business located here in Bellingham. At Erin Baker's, we are passionate about baking the healthy way. By using only the freshest wholesome ingredients we are able to create all natural products of exceptional quality. Everything we make is baked to order ensuring homemade freshness and great taste, perfect for life on the go. Breakfast is the most important meal of the day, what better way to begin your day than with Erin Baker's?

3 oz unsweetened chocolate (chopped)
1 can beets
½ cup butter (soft)
2½ cup brown sugar
3 large eggs (room temp)
2 tsp vanilla
2 cups flour
2 tsp baking soda
½ tsp salt
½ cup buttermilk

Chocolate buttercream frosting:
6 tbsp butter
1 cup powdered sugar
4 tbsp cocoa
2 to 3 tbsp milk

1. Preheat oven to 350°F.

2. Melt chocolate in glass bowl in microwave 60 seconds, remove and stir until smooth.

3. Puree beets in food processor.

4. Cream butter, eggs and vanilla in the bowl of electric mixer until incorporated and fluffy. Add pureed beets and melted unsweetened chocolate to the creamed mixture. Mix until well incorporated.

5. Sift together flour, baking soda and salt.

6. Add to creamed mixture the flour mixture and buttermilk alternating until all is incorporated and smooth. (Note: you will see the beet pieces...not to worry they will not be detected! I fool people all the time!)

7. Bake in one large 8 x 11 rectangular baking pan or two 8 inch spring form pans or this recipe makes 12 large cupcakes as well. Baking times vary from 25 min for cupcakes to 30 min for two cake pans to 35 min for 1 large pan. Cake is done when you insert a tooth pick and it comes out clean.

Chocolate buttercream frosting:

1. Cream butter.

2. Sift sugar and cocoa together.

3. Add cocoa mixture to butter.

4. Add milk to the butter mixture. I would start with 2 tbsp of milk and if it's too thick add another tbsp of milk.

"...This beet cake is the recipe that really got me started into baking. Even now, it is still one of my favorites. It really proves that you can change your food, change your life."
Erin Baker, founder

2 DIPPING SAUCES:
ORANGE JALAPENO & LEMON DILL

If eating super tasty fish and chips served from a refurbished London double decker bus is your thing, then you are in luck! But this Fairhaven icon isn't just for fish and chips. They have enlarged the menu to include seafood and soup and sandwich specials on a daily basis. They also boast 49 flavors of soft serve ice cream and during summer months they put out over 100 ice cream cones a day.

Orange Jalapeno:
12 oz orange marmalade
2 oz diced jalapeno peppers
½ tbsp granulated garlic
1 tbsp paprika
1 tbsp fresh lemon juice
Add ½ cup water to thin slightly (optional)

Lemon Dill:
½ cup mayonnaise
Juice of one lemon
2 tbsp chopped fresh dill
¼ tsp granulated garlic

Orange Jalapeno Dipping Sauce/Marinade:

A great dipping sauce for coconut prawns, scallops, deep fried shrimp and chilled shrimp. Also works well as a marinade for pork chops and chicken or as a sauce over cooked meatballs for a potluck.

Combine all ingredients in sauce pan, bring to simmer 20 minutes, do not boil. Chill before serving or serve hot.

Lemon Dill Sauce:

This sauce is the perfect complement to Salmon, Halibut, Cod or Dover Sole

Simply combine all ingredients in a bowl and serve!

"In the hands of an able cook, fish can become an inexhaustible source of perpetual delight."
Jean-Anthelme Brillat-Savarin (1755-1826)

HUNGARIAN BEEF GULYAS (GOULASH) SOUP

Fino is a famous style of dry sherry from southern Spain. It is also the name of the waterfront restaurant and wine bar located in the Chrysalis Inn in historic Fairhaven. People come to Fino to listen, to take in the harbor views, relax, sip, and taste in stylish and comfortable surroundings. But you must forget pretense, ceremony, and puffery – this is a place for wine drinkers, not wine snobs.

¼ cup flour (optional)
3 lbs trimmed beef, ½" dice
¼ cup vegetable oil
¼ cup unsalted butter
2 medium onions, small dice
1 red bell pepper, small dice
1 tbsp chopped garlic
2 tbsp mild paprika
1 tbsp hot paprika
½ tbsp thyme
½ tbsp caraway
2 Roma tomatoes, chopped
2 oven dried tomatoes, chopped
3 quarts beef stock
1½ lbs potatoes – small dice
¼ - ½ pounds veal or beef demiglace (optional)

1. Toss the diced beef in the flour (this is optional – to create a thicker soup).

2. In a large pot, brown the beef in oil and butter. Remove the beef and cook the onions & garlic in the same oil until a little soft. Add the spices and cook for two minutes. Add the tomatoes, peppers and stock and bring to a simmer.

3. Simmer for up to 2 hours, partially covered. Add a little water if it seems too thick.

4. Add the potatoes and cook for 10 minutes.

5. Stir in the optional demi-glace for richness.

6. Salt to taste. Ladle into bowls. Serve with sour cream on top.

"...Add a bottle of deep, rich Cabernet and you will get a symphony of flavors out of this dish ..."
Mick August, Owner

POLENTA PIE

In Roman times, polenta was the staple of the mighty Roman Legions. Even though bread was widely available in ancient Rome, the legions and the poor alike preferred the simplicity and taste of their early polenta. Maize was a perfect match for the farms of Northern Italy, where landowners could grow vast fields of corn for profit. Amazingly, this simple act of greed on the part of landowners helped shape a major component of Italian cooking. From then on, most of Italy's polenta consumption was made from corn, which ranges in color from golden yellow to the Veneto's white polenta.

Signature Tastes of **BELLINGHAM**

½ lb yellow grits
½ lb ground beef
½ yellow onion, diced
½ can sliced black olives, 14 oz
½ can whole kernel corn, 14 oz
1 can Italian diced tomato, 8 oz
1 can tomato sauce, 8 oz
1 can sliced mushrooms, 8 oz
1 tsp Italian seasoning
1 tsp garlic salt
½ tsp black pepper
¼ cup shredded parmesan

1. Add grits to 10 cups salted boiling water, stirring constantly. Once cooked (5 minutes), pour hot polenta into a greased 9x9 glass baking dish, ½" thick.

2. Pour remainder of polenta into another greased 9x9 dish, about 2" thick. Place both dishes in refrigerator to cool completely.

Beef Filling:

1. Brown beef with garlic salt, pepper, onions and Italian seasoning. Drain.

2. Return to heat and add remaining ingredients except cheese. Heat and stir for 3-5 minutes.

3. Remove and cool to room temperature.

Assembly:

4. Carefully turn out 2" polenta cake to a cutting board. Cut into ⅜" wide strips.

5. Use strips to line the sides of the ½" polenta cake pan.

6. Add 1" of meat mixture to polenta pan and spread evenly. Cover mixture completely with remaining polenta strips.

7. Spread parmesan over top of polenta cake.

8. Bake at 275°F for 50 minutes or until top is browning.

9. Cut into squares to serve.

FIRESIDE MARTINI AND WINE BAR
416 WEST BAKERVIEW ROAD

"Abudanza!"
Pat Corcoran, General Manager

BRAISED LAMB SHANKS

Lamb is a staple in all Mediterranean cooking, especially for the Greeks. Prepared properly, lamb is a very tender meat and this recipe captures all the robust flavors that lamb has to offer. Patience is a key ingredient in this dish as you must roast the lamb for a good while in order to get the meat so tender that it falls right off the shank.

4 lamb shanks
4 diced celery sticks
2 diced carrots
1 large yellow diced onion
2 jumbo diced carrots
4 crushed garlic cloves
½ cup extra virgin olive oil
½ cup red wine
salt
Fresh ground pepper
3 Greek bay leaves
4 cups crushed tomatoes
4 cups water
1 skillet
1 roasting pan

1. Preheat oven to 350°F.

2. On the stove top, brown the lamb shanks in the large skillet using a ½ cup olive oil at a high temperature. Season with salt & fresh ground pepper to taste. Promptly remove the shanks and place into the roasting pan.

3. Deglaze the skillet with ½ cup red wine and remove from heat.

4. Add celery, carrots, onion & garlic to the shanks in the pan. Take the reduced wine from the skillet and pour over all the shanks & vegetables. Add 3 bay leaves and 4 cups of crushed tomatoes, distributing evenly throughout the pan. Slowly pour in 4 cups of water, then cover the pan and place into oven.

4. After 2 hours rotate the shanks in the sauce, making sure to taste the sauce at this point and add any additional salt & pepper to taste.

The lamb shanks should be ready after 3-3.5 hrs of total roasting time. A good indicator is once the meat starts to fall off the bone. Accompany this meal with some warm pita bread and your favorite vegetables or roasted potatoes.

FIVE COLUMNS
1301 E MAPLE STREET

"...This hearty meal reminds me of the good times growing up in Greece, when the whole village would gather in celebration and roast meat dishes for everyone to feast on. From our kitchen to yours ...Kali Orexi! (Bon Appetit!)"
Dimitri Christopoulos, Owner & Chef

DR. GREG BAKER SUPERINTENDENT, FATHER

My favorite recipe is a scrumptious hors d'ouevre I serve whenever we have guests over. A large bowl of **Guacamole Dip** *with colored chips provides everyone with a little something to hold them over until the barbeque is in full swing. With onion, tomato, and guacamole, it's a healthy first course. And with some serious Tabasco and garlic, it's one most people will remember for the rest of the week.*

Three ripe avocados
1 Walla Walla sweet onion
1 big juicy red tomato
8 shakes of Tabasco sauce
As many cloves of garlic as you can handle
½ lime
1 bag of corn tortilla chips — blue, red and yellow mix

1. Peel the avocados, take out the seed in each and put into a large mixing bowl.

2. Use a fork or potato masher to break up avocados.

3. Chop up onion and tomato into big chunks; throw into the bowl.

4. Filter the garlic cloves through a garlic press into the bowl.

5. Cut the lime in half and squeeze ½ a lime into the bowl.

6. Put at least 8 full shakes of Tabasco into the bowl.

7. At this point, give the guacamole a taste and determine if you can handle more garlic and/or Tabasco.

8. Dump chips into another bowl, set both bowls on the counter, and let the fun begin!

Some say that the first tapa was simply a hunk of bread which was placed over a glass to keep the flies out - tapa literally meaning 'cover' or 'lid'. Thankfully tapas have progressed over the ages and now represent a culinary sensation of experiencing different tastes in the same meal. Spanish tapas-style dining is about having fun, sharing, eating your fill, and enjoying some good wine with friends. Flats house made creations offer the classic inspiration from Spain through the bounty of the Pacific Northwest.

Croquettes:
5 cups chicken stock
¼ cup saffron wine
1 small onion (small dice)
1 tbsp olive oil
1 pinch Saffron
2 cups Arborio rice
Salt to taste
½ tsp white pepper
1 tbsp butter
½ cup parmesan cheese
Chives sliced to garnish

8 oz Taleggio cheese (cut in ½ oz cubes)

Tomato Sauce:
2 tbsp roasted garlic oil
1 large onion (thinly sliced)
Pinch of salt
3 cloves roasted garlic
1 large can whole tomatoes
3 springs torn basil leaves
Salt and pepper to taste

Rice Mixture:

1. Saute onions in olive oil. Add rice, once rice is toasted, add saffron wine to deglaze pan.
2. Put chicken stock in separate pot and heat to simmer. Start to add chicken stock to rice until just covered with liquid, add saffron. Bring to simmer, cook rice till half the liquid is gone. Continue to add chicken stock slowly, 4 oz at a time, until rice is done and accepts no more liquid.
3. Add salt and pepper, stir in butter, add parmesan cheese and mix thoroughly. Cool, cover and wrap if necessary.

Preparing Croquettes:

1. Take 2½ oz of risotto and make flat in palm, place a cube of Taleggio cheese in center and roll into egg-like shape (keeping cheese in center). Repeat until all rice is used.
2. Place cookie sheet pans and freeze for one hour.

Tomato Sauce:

1. Slowly cook onions and garlic in olive oil and salt until onions are soft and sweet. Add tomatoes and simmer till sauce is rich and sweet stirring occasionally about 20 min.
2. Add torn basil leaves and season with salt and pepper. Strain mixture, removing all liquid. Discard solids.

Cooking and Serving:

1. Take flour, egg, and panko and place in separate pans.
2. Dust croquette with flour, place in egg, roll in panko.
3. Place 3 croquettes in deep fryer set at 360 – 375°F. Allow to cook until golden brown and hot all the way through.
4. Coat the bottom of a plate with Tomato Sauce, place 3 croquettes in a row, side by side. Garnish with chives.

"...I love tapas. They're like appetizers for a meal that never comes."
Marge Simpson

PENNE CON POLLO ALLA MESSINESE

The Italian people have few entertainment activities at night. So they spend most of their time on supper. Generally, the time for supper is very long from the starter to the pousse-cafe. You may want to sleep after you finish the supper. Sometimes, it can be midnight or the wee hours of the morning after you finish eating. But in no case will the Italian dependents rush the cook to serve food or strike a balance. They always like to have supper slowly and taste food with an easy and gentle mood.

2 lbs chicken breast, boneless, cubed
1 lb penne pasta
½ lb mushrooms
1 onion large, quartered and sliced
1 garlic clove, diced
½ cup dry white wine
1 cup heavy cream
¼ cup tomato sauce
1 cup arugula, rough chopped
3 tbsp parmesan cheese
3 tbsp gorgonzola cheese
Olive oil
Salt and pepper to taste

1. Add penne to salted boiling water to cook for 5-7 minutes. Remove and drain when pasta is al dente.

2. Sauté onions and garlic in olive for 2-3 minutes over a medium high heat.

3. Add mushrooms and chicken, and continue cooking for another 2-3 minutes. Chicken should be half-cooked at this point. Salt and pepper as desired.

4. Deglace pan with wine, then add cream and tomato sauce to create a rosé-coloured sauce.

5. Cook to reduce the sauce by ⅓, then add cheeses and arugula.

6. Cook for 1 minute and remove from heat.

7. Pour sauce over pasta and serve immediately.

"…The trouble with eating Italian food is that five or six days later you're hungry again."
George Miller

SPINACH PASTA SALAD

Based in Bellingham, Haggen was founded in 1933 and now operates 33 supermarkets in Washington and Oregon under the Haggen Food & Pharmacy and TOP Food & Drug names. Dedicated to providing their customers with the very best quality, their scratch-prepared products are made from recipes developed in-house.

5 cups rotini pasta
3 cups baby spinach
½ cup shredded parmesan
⅓ cup toasted pine nuts

Dressing:
¼ cup olive oil
½ cup golden balsamic vinegar
1 tbsp chopped garlic
1 tsp kosher or sea salt
1 tsp ground black pepper

1. Cook pasta to al dente, rinse with cold running water to cool down. Don't overcook as the pasta will break apart and be mushy.

2. Drain well and place in refrigerator to chill down.

3. For the dressing whisk all ingredients together well.

4. When pasta has chilled down combine all ingredients.

MULTIPLE BELLINGHAM LOCATIONS

HAGGEN

"...the best recipes always start with high quality ingredients..."
James Valentine, Corporate Executive Chef

COCONUT LIME SEAFOOD CHOWDER

Located in the Hotel Bellwether, the Harborside Bistro offers fresh seafood, locally grown vegetables, and fine aged meats prepared with artistry and care by their distinguished chefs. Combine that with a panoramic view of Bellingham Bay and the islands, and you'll never want to leave. In ten years, their signature Coconut Lime Seafood Chowder has only been off the menu once and had to be brought back due to customer demand. You could say it's pretty popular!

Base:
50 oz coconut milk
1 pint heavy cream
3 lemon grass stalks
3 chopped shallots
3 minced garlic cloves
1 quart chicken stock
¼ cup lime juice
¼ cup cilantro

Slurry:
Corn starch
Water

Seafood:
1 lb mussels
1 lb clams
1 lb salmon
1 lb halibut
1 lb scallops
1 lb shrimp

2 cups shiitake mushrooms

1. Bring all base ingredients to a boil, stirring constantly. Strain and discard the solids.

2. Mix together cornstarch and water to create the slurry. Add slurry to the base until you achieve the desired thickness.

3. Julienne slice the shiitake mushrooms.

4. Add seafood and shiitakes and cook until mussels and clams open up. Immediately remove from heat and serve - do not over cook!

5. Salt and pepper to taste. Garnish with some sesame seeds and tobiko caviar (optional).

At the restaurant they make this individually to order, but in the portions here, it will feed between 8 and 12, depending on their appetite.

HARBORSIDE BISTRO
ONE BELLWETHER WAY

"…My work has also motivated me to put a lot of time into seeking out good food and to spend more money for it."
Michael Pollan, author and chef

PUMPKIN SPICE COOKIES AND TOULOUSE SAUCE

The Harris Avenue Café exudes a warmth that immediately invites you in off of the streets of Fairhaven. Through the city's warmer months, you'll find folks enjoying their meals out in the quaint courtyard. A favorite of the Bellingham locals, the café is integrated with Tony's coffee and offers several breakfast and lunch times to catch your attention for many visits to come. We have two recipes...one for cookies, and one for a great sauce for eggs.

1 cup butter
½ cup white sugar
½ cup brown sugar
1 egg
1 tsp vanilla
1 cup pumpkin puree
1 tsp cinnamon
1 tsp ginger
½ tsp allspice
¼ tsp nutmeg
2 cups flour
1 tsp baking powder
1 tsp baking soda

1. Mix butter, white and brown sugar until fluffy.

2. Mix in egg and vanilla.

3. Add pumpkin, cinnamon, ginger, allspice and nutmeg. Cream completely, scraping sides often.

4. Sift flour, baking powder and baking soda, then add to mixture. Be careful not to over mix.

5. Place rounded scoops on baking sheet. Do not pat down.

6. Bake in oven at 325°F. Cool.

Toulouse Sauce:
½ bottle Champagne
1 cup white wine
1 cup half & half
20 oz cream cheese
6 oz tomato paste
½ tsp cayenne pepper
Zest and juice of ½ lemon
6 bay leaves

Toulouse Sauce (for eggs):

1. Heat Champagne in braising pan.

2. Add in wine and half & half.

3. Chunk cream cheese and add to the above mixture. Simmer.

4. Whisk in tomato paste, cayenne pepper and lemon. If mix is inconsistent, remove and puree.

5. Place in another pan to cool and leave uncovered.

6. Add bay leaves. Cool overnight in refrigerator.

HARRIS STREET CAFÉ
1415 RAILROAD AVENUE

"...One of the very nicest things about life is the way we must regularly stop whatever it is we are doing and devote our attention to eating...."
Luciano Pavarotti

CHICKEN FRIED STEAK

The Horseshoe Cafe is known for lots of things...It's hard not to be when you've been open 24 hours a day for nearly 125 years. But one thing we're known for is a great breakfast. It starts with Fresh Local Eggs, Scratch-Made Hash Browns and Hot Coffee. But that's just the basics...Add a hand-battered fried steak, country sausage gravy and that's breakfast Horseshoe-style.

Chicken Fried Steak:
2 cups flour
1 tbsp of parsley flakes
2 eggs
⅓ cup buttermilk
Salt and pepper to taste
Canola oil for frying

Country Sausage Gravy:
1 lb pork sausage
2 tbsp minced garlic
4 tbsp butter
1 cup milk
1 cup half & half
Ham bouillon
1 tsp sage
1 tsp thyme
4 tbsp flour
Salt and pepper to taste
Hot sauce to taste

1. Mix dry items and mix very well.

2. In a separate bowl mix eggs and buttermilk.

3. Pound steak as flat as possible to ensure it cooks even and thoroughly.

4. Dredge the steak in the flour mixture and dip in the egg mixture.

5. Repeat until thoroughly coated.

6. Deep fry or pan fry in canola oil (or other high-heat oil) until golden and thoroughly cooked.

7. Cook the minced sausage until lightly browned.

8. Add ham base, herbs, salt and pepper and simmer for 3-5 minutes.

9. Add butter, melt thoroughly then sprinkle flour and stir to create roux.

10. Stir constantly for 1 minute. Slowly add milk and cream stirring constantly until gravy reaches 165 °F.

11. Cook to desired thickness.

THE HORSESHOE CAFÉ
113 EAST HOLLY STREET

"...A great breakfast can start your day, end your night...or cure your hangover. We'll cook it fresh...you decide the rest..."
Michael Gonzalez , Horseshoe Cafe

CHICKEN KORMA

Korma has its roots in the Mughali cuisine of modern-day India. It is a characteristic Indian dish which can be traced back to the 16th century and to the Mughal incursions into present-day Northern India, Pakistan and Bangladesh. Classically, a korma is defined as a dish where meat or vegetables are braised with water, stock, and yoghurt or cream (the name is in fact derived from the Hindi and Urdu words for "braise"). The technique covers many different styles of korma.

¼ cup ghee or clarified butter
3 onions, chopped
½ cup water
1 tbsp ginger, grated
1 tbsp garlic, grated
2 tbsp cumin powder
2 tbsp cumin seed
½ tsp salt
½ tsp coriander seeds, crushed
2 tbsp coriander powder
Dash paprika
1 cup chicken stock
2 lbs chicken, chunked, boneless
¼ cup heavy cream
Dash garam masala
Chopped cilantro

1. Put ghee in a large skillet.

2. Add chopped onions and sauté on high heat until golden brown.

3. Stir in water, little by little.

4. Add all spices.

5. Cook for at least 2 minutes (texture will resemble gravy).

6. When mixture simmers, add chicken and stock.

7. Turn heat to medium high and add cream.

8. Cook 5-10 minutes until chicken is tender.

9. Remove from heat and season with cilantro and garam masala to taste.

INDIA GRILL
1215 CORNWALL AVENUE

"...This [recipe] is a cross between a few recipes I've used over the years...with other tweaks here and there. This is the closest to my favourite curry version..."
Jamie Oliver, celebrity chef and restauranteur

OWNER'S FAVORITE

It began one day as a young man strolled the streets of his hometown of Monterrey, Mexico. Jesse Cantu took in the intoxicating aromas of food being prepared in the cafes and noticed that no matter what life brought to people, it was the simple pleasures that gave them joy. The food and atmosphere of his youth inspired him to bring that same enjoyment to Jalapeno's customers. As in Mexico, we celebrate life and family with the simple pleasures.

½ lb skirt steak
½ onion, sliced
½ bell pepper, sliced
2 tbsp vegetable oil
4 jumbo prawns, shelled
4 pieces bacon
½ cup mozzarella cheese
Garlic, salt & pepper to taste
2 tbsp sour cream
2 tbsp guacamole
4 flour tortillas

1. Sauté vegetables in oil until tender. Set aside.

2. Season steak with garlic salt and pepper.

3. Over a hot charcoal grill, grill steak to a medium rare temperature (2-4 minutes each side) and remove to rest.

4. Meanwhile, microwave bacon for 2 minutes.

5. Wrap shrimp in bacon and grill for 1 minute each side.

6. Place steak in a broiler pan, adding peppers and onions to the top.

7. Lay the shrimp across the steak, and cover liberally with cheese.

8. Broil until cheese starts to brown.

9. Serve immediately with sour cream, guacamole, and flour tortillas.

JALAPENO'S
501 WEST HOLLY STREET

"...Have You Had Your BIG MAMA Today?"
Slogan for Jalapeno's Big Mama margarita. After a couple, you won't care how big she is.

BELLINGHAM BETTIES MISTRESSES OF MAYHEM

A Look in the Cupboard of...

Original Roller Derby was created by Leo Seltzer back in the 1930s. The first-ever Derby "game" was skated on August 13, 1935 in the Chicago Coliseum, with over 20,000 people watching. Bellingham Roller Betties was founded in 2006 as a skater owned and operated DIY, nonprofit organization and is now over 50 women strong. We're currently practicing, training and working together to build a roller-derby empire in the upper-left corner of the lower 48. The teams in Bellingham are: The Cog Blockers, FLASH, and Tough Love, and are overseen by the Refs.

So what do you feed the women warriors of Bellingham? What fuels the fire to take out your opponent? In a special segment, we took this question to them...in their own words.

Cat Scrap Fever (Cog Blockers): **beer can chicken**
Walker Texas Mangl'her (Tough Love): **blow pops**
Pearl Haggard (Cog Blockers): **anything you eat with chopsticks**
I.L. Kuttabetch (F.L.A.S.H.): **grilled peanut butter sandwich**
Chaos Fury (Tough Love): **crab ravioli with vodka cream sauce**
Eva Apocalypse (Cog Blockers): **tacos**
Mince Meatouttaya (Tough Love): **enchiladas with whole beans, cheese and white onions**
Beretta Garbo (F.L.A.S.H.): **perogis**
Ivonna Breakbones (F.L.A.S.H.): **pizza**
Luna Tick (Cog Blockers): **sauerkraut casserole**
D'Luca Brassie (Cog Blockers): **peaches**
Frosty Muggo Rootbeer (F.L.A.S.H. coach): **artichokes**
Fraid Knot (Cog Blockers): **asparagus**
Astro Glide (transfer from Rat City/yet to be drafted!): **Hotate (scallop sashimi)**
Lady Blackheart (Tough Love): **anything asian as long as it doesn't have dairy**

Thank you ladies. We will be watching your matches with rapt attention.

Signature Tastes of **BELLINGHAM**

deli by day – ALE & WINE BY NIGHT
Jeckyl & Hyde

WOOD FIRED PIZZAS
ALL SELECTIONS AVAILABLE AS CALZONE 11.95

- FOUR CHEESE 11.95
- AEGEAN – WHITE SAUCE, ONIONS, KALAMATA, CHEE...
- IONIAN – RED SAUCE, PEPPERONI, SALAMI, &FETA CHEESE 15.95
- SOPPRESSATA, &CANADIAN BACON 17.95
- TUSCAN – RED SAUCE, SALAMI, ARTICHOKES, GA...
- KALAMATA OLIVES, RED ONION, &CHEESE 16...
- SARDINIAN – GARLIC, SUNDRIED TOMATO, PEST...
- ONION, MUSHROOMS, & SOPPRESSATA 16.9...
- VEGETARIAN – SAUCE, RED BELL PEPPER, S...
- ARTICHOKE HEARTS, MUSHROOMS, ONION &OU...
- PACIFIC ISLANDER CHOICE OF SAUCE, SOPPR...
- CANADIAN BACON, PINEAPPLE, & CHEESE
- CHICKEN GARLIC... SAUCE, GARLIC, CH...
- SPINACH, ART... RED PEPPERS &ON...

HOT WOOD FIRED SANDWICHES
COMES WITH POTATO SALAD, COLESLAW,
TABOULE, OR GARDEN SALAD, SUBSTITUTION
OF BAKED TOFU FOR MEAT IS AVAILABLE.

- REUBEN - TRADITIONAL 7.95
- FRENCH DIP - CHOICE OF CHEESE 7.95
- ITALIAN PEPPERONI, SALAMI, SOPPRESSATA, RICOTTA,
  BLK OLIVES, TOMATOES & PESTO ON FOCCACIA 7.95
- MEDITERRANEAN - HUMMUS, TOMATO ON FOCCACIA 7.95
- ONIONS, SPINACH
- SOUTHWEST- SMOKED TURKEY, MONTEREY JACK,
  JALAPENOS, &GUACAMOLE ON CIABATTA 7.95
- GREEK - TURKEY, FETA, ROASTED RED PEPPERS,
  OLV TAPANADE, SPINACH ON CIABATTA 7.95
- CALIFORNIA TURKEY- TURKEY BACON, LETTUCE, TOMATO,
  & GUACAMOLE & MAYO ON FOCCACIA 7.95

COLD DELI SANDWICHES
COMES WITH PICKLE AND LAYS POTATO CHIPS
FULL 6.75   HALF 4.50
SELECT 2 MEAT, 1 CHEESE, BREAD, & TOPPINGS

BREADS   MEATS: CHEESES:
MULTI GRAIN   TURKEY   CHEDDAR/SWISS
WHITE   SMKD TURKEY   PEPPERJACK
WHEAT   BLK HAM   PROVOLONE
MARBLE RYE   ROAST BEEF   SMKD GOUDA
SOUR DOUGH   SALAMI   MONTEREY JACK
HOAGIE ROLL   CORNED BEEF   CREAM CHEESE

FOCCACIA
CIABATTA
GLUTEN FREE

TOPPINGS: MAYO
LETTUCE   MUSTARD/DIJON
TOMATO   OIL/VINEGAR
PICKLES   HORSERADISH
ONIONS   1000 ISLAND
CUCUMBERS   PESTO add .75
BLACK OLIVES   TAPANADE add .75
MUSHROOMS

SPECIALTY
SANDWICHES

VEGGIE 6.00
VEGGIE HUMMUS WRAP 6.50

DRESSINGS

CHEF LUNCH 8.00 DINNER 9.00
CHICKEN CAESAR LUNCH 8.00 DINNER 9.00
SESAME CHICKEN LUNCH 8.00 DINNER 9.00
GARDEN SIDE 3.95 ENTREE 6.50

LOOK TO THE LEFT for SPECI...
QUICHE w/ SOUP OR SALAD 6.50
½ SANDWICH w/SOUP OR SALAD 7.50
CUP OF SOUP & SALAD 6.95
SOUP w/ FOCCACIA   BOWL 5.85   CUP 3.00
CHILI w/ CORNBREAD BOWL 5.85   CUP 3.00

We use Compostible Take...

4 LG. SODA

VEGGIE TOPP...
- KALAMATA
- BLACK OLIVE
- MUSHROO...
- RED PEPPE...
- TOMATO...

LISA'S POTATO SALAD

Signature Tastes of BELLINGHAM

At J & H, as its known to regular customers, there is a little bit of a day and night transition. A mild-mannered delicatessen by day, anchoring lunch-time working folks traffic with hearty sandwiches, J & H slips into an alter ego at night, with substantial offerings of wine, hand-crafted beers, and their wood-fired pizzas. The food will draw you in, and the entertainment, from drawing on the tables, car-shows and live music, will keep you coming back for more of this dichotomy in a deli.

8 Idaho baking potatoes
2 cups celery, chopped
2 cups white onions, chopped
½ cup olive oil
Salt and pepper to taste
12 eggs, hardboiled and chopped
8 dill pickles, chopped
3 cups mayonnaise

There is a technique that has to be used to achieve the salad's best taste. Keep the potato part of the salad separate from the wet part of the salad in a fridge for about an hour or two, then combine to make the best potato salad you have ever tasted. This lets the spices get into the onions and potatoes, for better flavor. The potatoes are baked, not boiled. So lets get started..

Bake 8 to 10 Idaho baking potatoes, in an oven at 350 degrees for 40 to 50 minutes, just so the potatoes are just getting soft. Let cool 20 minutes, then peel the skins off and chop into cubes. (around 1 inch square or a little smaller.. Add 2 cups chopped celery, and 2 cups chopped up white onions. Add ½ cup of good olive oil, salt and pepper to taste. Mix well and put in the fridge.

Now to make the dressing part of the salad.......

Chop 12 - 15 hard boiled eggs, 8 dill pickles chopped into tiny pieces and 3 cups of mayonnaise. Mix together thoroughly and cool in fridge for a while. After both parts are cold, Mix the potato mixture with the mayo mixture together. Add more mayonnaise, salt and pepper to taste if needed. Salad should be creamy and not dry. Other spices can be added if your personal preference requires it. Otherwise the salad is complete and will please any crowd.

When serving, place a little dry dill on top for a little taste and a good presentation. Good luck and remember not to mix together until a few hours later.

"..."With every day, and from both sides of my intelligence, the moral and the intellectual, I thus drew steadily nearer to the truth, by whose partial discovery I have been doomed to such a dreadful shipwreck: that man is not truly one, but truly two..."

Robert Louis Stevenson, Dr. Jekyll and Mr. Hyde

Maple Pumpkin Cupcakes

Katie's Cupcakes is all about serving little cakes of happiness. Katie's bakes their cupcakes from scratch every morning and uses only the best ingredients. There are hundreds of flavors just waiting to be created. Katie's Cupcakes is a great place to bring your kids or just relax with a cup of tea. They offer cupcakes for any event, baby showers, birthday parties and weddings.

2 cups sugar
1¼ cups oil
1 tsp vanilla
2 cups pumpkin
4 eggs
2 cups flour
½ tsp nutmeg
½ tsp ginger
½ tsp cloves
2 tsp cinnamon
1 tbsp baking powder
2 tsp baking soda
¼ tsp salt

Maple buttercream:
2 cups butter
3 cups powdered sugar
2 tsp maple extract
1 tbsp heavy cream

1. In a medium sized bowl sift together flour, nutmeg, ginger, cloves, cinnamon, baking powder, baking soda and salt.

2. In large bowl mix together sugar and oil with mixer. Add vanilla and pumpkin and mix well.

3. Gradually add flour mixture to the pumpkin mixture until combined. Do not over mix.

Maple buttercream:

1. In a mixer, combine butter and sugar.

2. Add the cream and maple extract.

3. Mix on medium speed until smooth and creamy.

Makes about 24-30 cupcakes.

KATIE'S CUPCAKES
1005 HARRIS AVENUE

"...creating fabulous cupcakes is about not being afraid to try new things..."
Lynn Rovelstad, Owner and Founder

CALIFORNIA ROLL

We can trace sushi's origin back to the 4th century BC in Southeast Asia. As a preserved food, the salted fish, fermented with rice, was an important source of protein. The cleaned and gutted fish were kept in rice so that the natural fermentation of the rice helped preserve the fish. This type of sushi is called nare-zushi, and was taken out of storage after a couple of months of fermentation, and then only the fish was consumed while the rice was discarded.

Signature Tastes of BELLINGHAM

Juice of ½ lemon
1 medium avocado, peeled, pitted, and sliced into ¼" thick pieces
4 sheets nori (seaweed paper)
2 cups steamed rice, cooled
⅓ cup sesame seeds, toasted
1 small cucumber, peeled, seeded, and cut into match-stick-size pieces
4 crabsticks, torn into pieces

Squeeze the lemon juice over the avocado to prevent browning.

1. Cover a bamboo rolling mat with plastic wrap.

2. Cut nori sheets in half crosswise. Lay 1 sheet of nori, shiny side down, on the plastic covered mat.

3. Wet your fingers with water and spread about ½ cup of the rice evenly onto the nori.

4. Sprinkle the rice with sesame seeds. Turn the sheet of nori over so that the rice side is down.

5. Place ⅛ of the cucumber, avocado and crab sticks in the center of the sheet.

6. Grab the edge of the mat closest to you, keeping the fillings in place with your fingers, and roll it into a tight cylinder, using the mat to shape the cylinder.

7. Pull away the mat and set aside.

8. Cover with a damp cloth. Repeat until all of the rice has been used.

9. Cut each roll into 6 pieces.

KURU KURU SUSHI
STE 101, 11 BELLWETHER WAY

"…And I find chopsticks frankly distressing. Am I alone in thinking it odd that a people ingenious enough to invent paper, gunpowder, kites and any number of other useful objects, and who have a noble history extending back 3,000 years haven't yet worked out that a pair of knitting needles is no way to capture food?"
Bill Bryson, author

TOMATO BASIL SOUP

Four thousand years ago people built fires in small caves in order to cook food. At La Fiamma the cave has been transformed into an oven, but real wood fire remains the sole source of heat. Apple wood, gleaned from the vast orchards of the Yakima Valley, fuels the fire of our oven. When burned, this wood produces an intense, consistent heat, while also imparting a sumptuous aroma. Our oven creates the ultimate environment for true artisan wood fire pizza. Thus our name, La Fiamma — the Flame! From pepperoni to Moo Shu, one taste and you'll understand why in 6000 years wood fire cooking has never gone out of style

2 tbsp olive oil
2 medium onions, diced
¼ cup chopped garlic
½ lb fennel bulb sliced
1 serrano chili, minced
1 tsp fennel seed ground
2 tbsp burgundy vinegar
2 tbsp brown sugar
1 tbsp salt
1½ tsp black pepper
1 cup red wine
1 qt vegetable stock
(3) 28 oz cans ground tomatoes
(Muir Glen Organic)
¾ cup heavy cream
2 tbsp basil pesto

1. In a large stock pot, sauté first 6 ingredients together.
2. When veggies are translucent add burgundy wine vinegar, brown sugar, salt, black pepper, red wine and vegetable stock.
3. Cook for approximately twenty minutes.
4. Gather three cans of tomatoes. Add to pot and cook for two hours. Keep a long handled spoon handy for stirring.
5. Add heavy cream and cook an additional thirty minutes.
6. Remove from heat. Strain soup through a fine mesh strainer.
7. Stir in basil pesto, serve or store.

"…I live on good soup, not on fine words."
Moliere

SMALL COOKIES
.95 ea

Mushroom Barley Soup

"The life in pink" or simply "The Good Life". Established in 1997, La Vie en Rose is family owned and operated and a true scratch bakery. From our cakes to our display case, we add love and a personal touch to all that we do. Our small staff works to make our bakery warm and inviting, spoiling our customers with beautiful food, splendid drinks and a peaceful atmosphere.

1 lb pearl barley
½ lb mushrooms, sliced
4 large carrots, diced
3 tbsp vegetable base
2 qt water
1 cup boiling water
Salt and pepper to taste

1. Rinse pearl barley and place in a stock pot with water.

2. Dissolve the vegetable base into the boiling water, stirring to mix completely.

3. Add the hot water with base to the stock pot.

4. Slowly heat to simmer, and allow to simmer for 20 minutes.

5. Add the mushrooms and carrots.

6. Continue simmering until the soup thickens.

7. Salt and pepper to taste.

8. Refrigerate the leftovers. You might need to add more water when the soup is reheated.

La Vie en Rose
111 WEST HOLLY STREET

"…[Breadbaking is] one of those almost hypnotic businesses... It leaves you filled with one of the world's sweetest smells... there is no chiropractic treatment, no Yoga exercise, no hour of meditation in a music-throbbing chapel, that will leave you emptier of bad thoughts than this homely ceremony of making bread."
M.F.K. Fisher, The Art of Eating

MAPLE BUTTERMILK BARS

Did you ever wonder where the first doughnut recipes originated? Well, believe it or not, the Bible's Old Testament records in Leviticus 7:12 that the priest offered with the sacrifice of thanksgiving "...cakes mingled with oil, of fine flour, fried." Sounds like a doughnut to me! Now, the exact recipe is a Lafeen's trade secret, but this home recipe will fill the craving for when Lafeen's is closed!

2 cups sugar
1 cup of buttermilk
3 eggs
1 tbsp butter
3 tsp baking powder
6 cups flour
½ tsp nutmeg
1 tsp cinnamon

Maple Frosting:
¼ cup shortening
½ tsp salt
¼ cup maple syrup
2 tsp vanilla
3 cups confectioners' sugar
¼ cup milk

Bars

1. Combine all dry ingredients in a large bowl.

2. Mix wet ingredients in another bowl.

3. Alternately combine dry ingredients with wet in a mixer.

4. Once mixed, place the batter on the dusting flour.

5. Spread the batter evenly to form a ½" thick piece of dough.

6. Now, cut the batter with a bar cutter. It should make 16 bars.

7. Use a scraper to slightly cut each bar lengthwise. Brush the flour off the bars and put them on a screen to be deep fried.

8. Fry the bars in soybean oil at 300°F for 4 minutes. Flip the bars over so that the cut sides are facing down.

9. Frost the buttermilk bars to your liking.

Frosting

1. Combine shortening, salt, syrup, vanilla and 1 cup of sugar.

2. Add milk and remaining sugar alternately.

3. Mix until smooth and creamy. Add more sugar to thicken or milk to thin, if needed for good spreading consistency.

" ...Be sweet and honest always, but God's sake, don't eat my doughnuts!"
Emma Bunton, British singer

GOUDA CHICKEN

This intimate, artistic restaurant overlooks Fairhaven from the historic Sycamore Square building. It offers an eclectic blend of comfort food and upscale cuisine with European influences, which is both delicious and reasonably priced. The food and service is complemented by the dark, mysterious atmosphere.

1½ chicken breast, boneless
1 cup heavy cream
2 oz bay shrimp
1 cup Gouda cheese, shredded
⅛ cup of pesto
2 oz of dry sherry

This recipe is for one serving. However it is easy to make this dish for a family of four or more, to do so adjust the proportions accordingly. As a staff and customer favorite, this dish will soon be one of your favorites too, we hope, cheers and happy cooking!

1. Pre- heat the oven to 400°F.

2. Either use a large ramekin dish that will fit the chicken, or use a cast iron skillet which will work better if you are making more than one serving.

3. Pour a ¼ cup of the heavy cream into dish. Add a ¼ cup of the shredded Gouda.

4. Put the 2 oz of bay shrimp in the pan next and then place the chicken breast on top covered with the rest of the cheese.

5. Cover the dish and put it in the oven for 8 minutes.

Sauce

1. Put the rest of the heavy cream, pesto and sherry into a pan on the stove top to simmer.

2. Stir well until hot, the color should be a light green.

3. Take the chicken out of the oven after the 8 minutes.

4. Take off the cover and put it back in for 3-5 minutes to crisp the cheese on top.

5. After the cheese is crispy enough, take the dish and plate it, ensuring that there is enough shrimp per portion. Then cover the chicken with the pesto sauce and Viola! Enjoy!

LE CHAT NOIR
1200 HARRIS AVENUE

"…At 'The Black Cat' we love good food and good friends, but keep in mind that good food takes time to make. Coming to our establishment is like walking into the old television show Cheers, ' where everyone knows your name'…"

CRAB CAKE OMELET

The Little Cheerful is a breakfast and lunch cafe located conveniently in a restaurant on the corner of Railroad Avenue. and Holly Street. in beautiful downtown Bellingham. We are well known for our sense of style, sauciness and general good looks, as well as for our (often) delicious food and our (above average) service. We were recently featured in Sunset magazine and will be featured in an upcoming Cosmopolitan questionnaire "Best places to eat breakfast following a night of debauchery and the often inevitable 'walk of shame'."

6 celery stalks, finely chopped
2 red onions, finely chopped
3 red bell peppers, finely chopped
2 jalapeno peppers, diced
Juice of 1 lemon
6 eggs
7 cloves of garlic, diced
2 tbsp red pepper flakes
2 tbsp parsley flakes
1 tbsp dill
1 tbsp stone ground mustard
1 tbsp yellow mustard
2 tbsp mayonnaise
10 lbs crab meat
Panko bread crumbs to coat

Omelet
2 tbsp butter
¼ cup Monterey Jack cheese, shredded
3 eggs, scrambled
½ avocado, sliced into strips
¼ cup pico de gallo

Crab cakes

1. Mix all ingredients except crab well.

2. Fold in crab meat, until ingredients are incorporated.

3. Form into round patties 3" in diameter.

4. Gently bread patties in panko mix.

5. Place on a baking sheet and refrigerate overnight.

Omelet

1. Melt butter over medium high heat.

2. Fry 2 crab cakes on both sides until browned.

3. Drain and set aside.

4. Melt 1 tbsp butter to a skillet over medium high heat.

5. Add eggs, pulling ¼ of the edges toward the center after 15 seconds.

6. Continue pulling remaining edges.

7. Add cheese to the omelet and place in a 375°F degree oven to finish (2-4 minutes).

8. Remove from oven and add crab cakes to omelet.

9. Fold over ½ of omelet and top with avocado and pico de gallo.

10. Serve immediately.

"...Eat at the Little Cheerful. If you don't, who will?"
Missy May, Goddess Incarnate of Little Cheerful

POLISH BAKED DUMPLINGS WITH SPINACH AND CHEESE

The French do not have a monopoly on crepes. While the French version is something most people are familiar with, the art of wrapping a thin pancake around sweet or savory foods is a celebrated European tradition with several variations, from the "pfannkuchen" in Germany to "naleśniki" in Poland. For owners Magdalena and Greg Theisen, Magdalena's Creperie in Fairhaven is a perfect forum for showcasing Magda's mastery of European delights.

Dough:
1 cup milk
1 tsp sugar
2 tbsp instant dry yeast
3 cups flour
¼ lb butter, melted
Salt to taste

Filling:
1 lb fresh spinach
1 tbsp oil for frying
½ lb feta or any white cheese
2 tbsp fresh grated parmesan cheese
2 crushed garlic cloves
1 tbsp sour cream
Pinch of pepper and nutmeg
Salt to taste

Glaze:
1 egg lightly beaten
Herbs (Italian herb mix, for instance cumin, red pepper flakes, sea salt)

Making the Dough:

1. Warm milk (to encourage yeast growth, not too hot), pour into a bowl, stir in the sugar until it dissolves and stir in the yeast with a wooden spoon.

2. Mix in the flour, and finally mix in the butter. Mix until you have a smooth dough.

3. Cover with a damp cloth and leave to rise for 30 min.

Preparing the Filling:

1. Fry spinach about 1 minute in 1 tbsp of oil. Add the remaining ingredients and mix.

Make the Dumplings:

1. Roll out the dough to about ⅛" thick. Using a juice glass approx 2" dia, cut circles from the dough.

2. Take one of the circles and place a spoonful of filling on it. Fold the edges together over the filling to make a crescent moonshape and pinch the edges together. If you leave even a small hole in the edges, they will open up during baking so pinch them closed very carefully.

3. Put dumplings onto a cookie sheet lined with baking paper, leaving a small space between them as they will grow some during rising and baking. Let stand in warm draft free place for 15 minutes to rise.

4. Preheat oven to 400°F. Baste the dumplings with the egg mixture and sprinkle with herbs.

5. Bake 10-15 minutes until lightly browned. Serve hot from the oven with dipping sauce.

Other filling combinations you may also like: lentils and mushrooms, sauerkraut and mushrooms, lentils with bacon and ham. The best way to serve is with a dipping sauce, i.e. horseradish sauce, blue cheese sauce or garlic sauce. Enjoy your meal!

MAGDALENA'S CREPERIE
1200 10TH STREET, SUITE 103

"...I have a passion for cooking and I love to eat...Just like that, the idea was born. We wanted to create something that is a little unique and difficult to find in this area. It's very European."

Magdalena Theisen, Owner

DR. MICHAEL SULLIVAN E.R. PHYSICIAN

*Working in the Emergency Department at St. Joseph's Hospital, I don't have a great deal of time for cooking. Well, for much of anything for that matter. And you would think that with my fine Irish heritage, I would crave Corned Beef and Cabbage. To be honest, I ate it so much as a kid that I can hardly stand the smell of it now. So give me a big **Barbeque Pulled Pork** sandwich, and I am happy. Best of all, I don't have to sit down to eat it.*

Barbeque Rub
½ cup brown sugar
¼ cup paprika
1 tbsp salt
1 tbsp black pepper
1 tbsp chili powder
1 tbsp garlic powder
1 tbsp celery salt
1 tsp cayenne pepper

3-5 lb. Boston Butt pork roast, preferably bone-in

1 cup barbeque sauce

1. Dry off pork with paper towels and discard.

2. Rub pork liberally with Barbeque Rub. If you need more, make more!

3. Place in a crock pot and cook on Low 6 hours. I've been late about by about 6 hours and it has been fine to eat!

4. Remove lid and pour off most of the excess liquid (there will be quite a bit to discard).

5. Pour on the BBQ sauce and mix in well with a fork (this is also what breaks up the meat). Enjoy!

Signature Tastes of BELLINGHAM

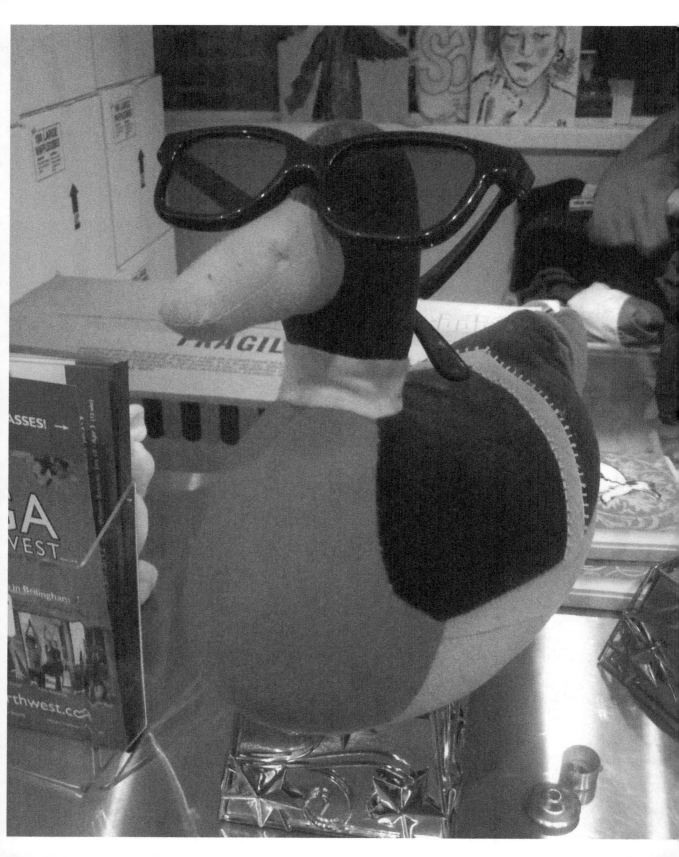

FUDGE SAUCE

Welcome to Mallard Ice Cream where we beg the question...could ice cream really be the food of the gods? It's reasonable to assume that ambrosia, food of the gods, was organic. Here at Mallard we hand craft ice cream with an emphasis on fresh, local, organic ingredients. What we do is deceptively simple, and while we do our best to stick to the basics, we encourage you to look around and see how we turn something simple into something blatantly superior.

1¼ cup sugar
¼ cup + 1 tbsp milk
1 cup cream
¼ lb cocoa mass
¼ lb cocoa powder
1 tsp vanilla

1. Combine sugar, milk, cream in saucepan on med-high heat. Pan should be large enough to leave lots of room to whisk in dry ingredients.

2. Bring to just-boiling and remove from heat.

3. Whisk in the Cocoa first. Make sure most of the lumps are dissolved. A hand mixer can also be used to get it smooth.

4. Then stir in the cocoa mass.

5. Add the vanilla last.

If the sauce is too thick, or if the sauce breaks (oil separates), thin with a tsp at a time of warm water. I find that if you thin the sauce with milk, it starts to taste like pudding, so water is better.

Cocoa Mass and high quality cocoa powder are available at Chocolate Necessities.

Signature Tastes of **BELLINGHAM**

MALLARD'S ICE CREAM
1323 RAILROAD AVENUE

"...Chocolate is a divine, celestial drink, the sweat of the stars, the vital seed, divine nectar, the drink of the gods, panacea and universal medicine."

Geronimo Piperni, quoted by Antonio Lavedán, Spanish army surgeon,1796

ZUCCHINI STEW

Mambo Italiano Café opened its doors back in 2001 and has been pleasing its patrons ever since. Situated in the Sycamore Square building, the restaurant is located in the very heart of historic Fairhaven. Owner and Executive Chef Sam Tino is a 2nd Generation Restaurateur who grew up in an Italian restaurant. Passion for food runs in the family. Chef Tino features several delicious family recipes as well as many distinctive seafood dishes.

3-4 zucchini, chopped 2"
pieces
3-4 large tomatoes, quartered
1 onion, diced
3 cloves garlic, minced
Bunch of fresh basil, torn up
Salt and pepper
2 eggs

1. Sauté the onion and garlic in olive oil until golden.
2. Sprinkle with salt and pepper.
3. Add the zucchini, tomatoes, and basil. Stir together.
4. Cover and put on low heat for 1.5 - 2 hours.
5. 10 minutes before eating, poach eggs in the liquid. Add more salt to taste.

This rustic Italian dish is perfect for the end of summer harvest. This stew is delicious, and exemplifies down home Italian cooking: the freshest ingredients prepared simply with love.

MAMBO ITALIANO
1303 12TH STREET

"And hey Mambo! Don't wanna tarantella,
Hey Mambo! No more-a moozzarella.
Hey Mambo! Hey Mambo Italiano.
Try an enchilada with a fish-a-barcalada."
Rosemary Clooney, "Mambo Italiano"

BREAKFAST BURRITO

The York District is a classic. One of the oldest neighborhoods in Bellingham, it boasts quality homes, mature landscaping, and a tight-knit community. Located just east of downtown, its nearly 3,000 residents enjoy the most unique parts of Bellingham. The neighborhood dates back to the late 1890's, with most of the homes being built in the early 20th century. Anchoring the community is Nelson's Market, with Marlin's Restaurant under Paul Ostby, tucked off Potter Street.

1½ lbs potatoes
¼ lb ham
2 oz bacon
¼ lb sausage
2 oz bell peppers
2 oz onions
2 oz mushroom
6 oz cheese
3 eggs
3 flour tortillas
2 tbsp oil

1. In a frying pan, fry up potatoes, ham, bacon, sausage, bell peppers, onions, and mushrooms until done.

2. Whisk eggs and dump into same pan.

3. In another pan toast the tortillas on both sides, then add cheese and ⅓ of eggs mix.

4. Wrap up like burrito and place back in pan on low to seal burrito.

MARLIN'S AT NELSON'S MARKET
514 POTTER STREET

"…I don't know how comfortable I am sharing a recipe and photos with you. I'm afraid of more folks loving it here and wanting to move in!"
Paul Ostby, chef of Marlin's

Tex-Mex Tacos

Food historians tell us TexMex cuisine originated hundreds of years ago when Spanish/Mexican recipes combined with Anglo fare. TexMex, as we Americans know it today, is a twentieth century phenomenon. Dictionaries and food history sources confirm the first print evidence of the term "Tex Mex" occured in the 1940s. Linguists remind us words are often used for several years before they appear in print. TexMex restaurants first surfaced ouside the southwest region in cities with large Mexican populations. Diana Kennedy, noted Mexican culinary expert, is credited for elevating this common food to trendy fare.

1 lb outside skirt steak or flat iron steak *vegetable oil* *¼ tsp garlic salt (to taste)* *fresh salsa or pico de gallo* *fresh lime (to taste)* *flour tortillas*	1. Grill steak until medium rare, remove and let stand 5 minutes. 2. Dice steak and place into a skillet with oil over a medium heat. 3. Add garlic salt and fresh salsa and stir for one minute. 4. Remove from heat and squeeze fresh lime juice over the steak and salsa mixture. 5. Spoon into warm flour tortillas and enjoy!

MILAGRO MEXICAN GRILL
1007 HARRIS AVENUE

"...Tex-Mex food might be described as native foreign food, contradictory through that term may seem, It is native, for it does not exist elsewhere; it was born on this soil. But it is foreign in that its inspiration came from an alien cuisine; that it has never merged into the mainstream of American cooking and remains alive almost solely in the region where it originated..."

Lapses of Judgement from <u>Eating in America</u>, Waverly Root & Richard de Rochemont 1976

GRILLED FLATBREAD PIZZA WITH FIGS, BACON, FETA AND ARUGULA

At Nimbus, great ingredients form the foundation of their cuisine, and strive to support local farmers and fishermen who supply the highest quality fresh ingredients for their globally influenced seasonal cuisine. Their culinary goal is to creatively utilize flavors, textures, aromas, and colors to engage the senses; providing their guests with an elevated dining experience.

Flatbread Dough:
1 tbsp active dry yeast
¼ cup warm water
2 tsp sugar
2 tsp Kosher salt
1 tbsp honey
2 tbsp extra virgin olive oil
2 cups bread flour

Fig Topping:
8 oz diced dried figs, de-stemmed
½ cup water
¼ cup sugar
½ cup port
1 lb fresh diced figs, de-stemmed

Other Toppings:
2 cups crumbled feta cheese
1 bunch arugula, leaves only
Sea salt
Fresh cracked black pepper
Extra virgin olive oil
Fresh figs, sliced
Crispy bacon

Flatbread Dough:

1. In electric mixer bowl, combine yeast and water and let stand 5 minutes or until yeast begins to bubble.

2. Combine sugar, salt and flour. Add to yeast mixture, mix on low speed. Add honey and olive oil, continue mixing 6 to 8 minutes until you have a smooth dough.

4. Place dough in large bowl, shape into a tight ball and coat with olive oil. Cover with a towel and set in a warm spot to rise. Dough should double in size.

5. Punch dough down; place on a floured work surface. Divide dough into 2 or 4 equal pieces and shape into round pizzas. Transfer pizzas to oiled cookie sheet.

6. Pre-heat a gas grill and brush with oil. Brush pizzas lightly with olive oil; carefully place on grill. Dough should immediately start to bubble. Use tongs to move dough. Cook on both sides to mark dough and partially cook. Transfer to cookie sheet to cool.

Fig Topping:

1. Combine dried figs with water, sugar and port; cook until tender and liquid has reduced slightly. Add fresh figs; cook on low to jam consistency, 10 minutes. Cool.

Assembling Pizza:

1. Spread fig topping on each pizza and arrange 4 fig slices over topping. Sprinkle with bacon and feta.

2. Bake directly on oven rack for 8 minutes or until cheese is melted and toppings are warm.

3. Remove from oven and top with arugula, sea salt, olive oil, and pepper. Serve immediately.

"…There is no love sincerer than the love of food"
George Bernard Shaw

the
oboe
cafe

A history…Sylvester Graham develops Graham flour and Graham Crackers; Dr. James C. Jackson uses sheets of baked Graham flour, broken up, rebaked and broken up again to create "Granula". Then Dr. John Harvey Kellogg, a director of a Battle Creek Sanitarium, develops a mix of baked whole grains, and also calls it "Granula"; is sued by Dr. Jackson, renames it Granola, but it never becomes a success. Along comes Charles W. Post, a patient at the Battle Creek Sanitarium, leaves uncured, gets cured by another group, opens his own health retreat, and makes his own Granola recipe, but calls it Grape Nuts and makes it commercially successful.

1 lb rolled oats
¾ lb slivered almonds
⅓ lb raw sunflower seeds
⅓ lb pumpkin seeds (Pepitas)
¼ lb white sesame seeds
¼ lb hazelnuts (Filberts)
¼ lb raw pistachios, shelled

1 cup honey
⅛ cup canola oil
2 tbsp brown sugar
2 tsp cinnamon
½ tsp ginger

1 tsp almond extract
1 tsp vanilla extract

2 cups Craisins
1 cup golden raisins
1 cup dark raisins
½ cup dried apricot slices

1. Mix together the first 7 ingredients and set aside.

2. In a tall sauce pan, bring honey with ginger to a boil.

3. Add the extracts and boil for another minute.

4. Pour honey mixture over ingredients that are set aside and stir carefully as the honey will be hot.

5. Spread evenly on cookie sheets and bake at 350°F until golden brown, approximately 15 minutes.

6. Once this is pulled from the oven add the dried fruit and stir together.

7. Let sit on the counter until completely cooled and store in an air tight container until ready to eat.

P.S. It is really hard not to eat it while it is still warm.

OBOE CAFÉ
714 LAKEWAY DRIVE

"…All happiness depends on a leisurely breakfast."
John Gunther, American journalist and author

BLUEBERRY COFFEE CAKE

The Old Town Cafe is a special place for many people, both customers and workers. The people who work here are a team. Many perform all the jobs from dishwasher and cook, to waitperson and manager. All jobs are equally important and dependent on the other, so tips are shared equally. We use many natural, local and organic products as possible and practical. Most item on our menu are made in our kitchen. All of our pastries are made here, many with whole wheat flour and unrefined sweetners.

1 cup butter, softened
2 cups sugar
6 eggs

Dry Mixture:
2 cups whole wheat pastry flour
3 cups white flour
1 tbsp baking powder
2 tsp baking soda
½ tsp salt
2 cups sour cream

Crumb topping:
1 cup brown sugar
1 cup white sugar
1 tsp cinnamon
½ cup butter, cold
½ cup chopped walnuts or pecans

2 cups of blueberries

Crumb Topping:

1. Mix all ingredients in a food processor.

2. Pulse until finely chopped.

3. Place in refrigerator to set butter.

Dry Mixture:

1. Combine all dry mixture ingredients.

2. Mix in an electric mixer, alternating dry mixture additions with sour cream until incorporated; Set aside.

3. Beat butter and sugar with a paddle-style mixer until fluffy (10 minutes).

4. Add eggs, one at a time, until smooth.

5. Fold sour cream batter into cake batter.

Assembly:

1. Grease a 8½"x11" pan.

2. Add half of batter to pan, spreading evenly.

3. Add blueberries evenly to batter.

4. Carefully pour remaining batter on top of blueberries and top with 3 cups of crumb mixture.

5. Bake at 350ºF for 1 hour or until done.

OLD TOWN CAFÉ
316 WEST HOLLY STREET

"…there are customers I see four or five times a week, some every day…It's kind of like home for both of us…"
Diane Brainard, Owner

Italian Tuna
Stuffed Pepperoncini

When Anna & Christos opened the deli in June of 2007 the wine rack was empty, there were six sandwiches on the menu and a little one on the way. With a lot of hard work, a baby, an expansion and a few more employees, Old World Deli has grown up a lot in the past few years. Give her a few more years and their daughter Mira will be taking orders and making soup alongside her Papa. With a deli counter a native New Yorker would be proud of, as well as an impressive wine and specialty food selection, there is so much more than meets the mouth…er, eye!

1 lg can Italian tuna, packed in olive oil
½ cup flat leaf parsley, chopped
½ tbsp red chile flakes
10 whole pepperoncini
Pinch of salt

1. Empty the tuna with olive oil into a bowl.

2. Break up the tuna until well mixed with olive oil.

3. Add the parsley, chili flakes and salt to taste.

4. Slit the pepperoncini under the stem and slice down halfway. Remove seeds and drain excess pickling vinegar.

5. Stuff the tuna mixture into the empty pocket of the pepperoncini.

6. Serve immediately. This is the perfect snack-bite or antipasti addition.

OLD WORLD DELI
1228 NORTH STATE STREET

"…In America, I would say New York and New Orleans are the two most interesting food towns. In New Orleans, they don't have a bad deli. There's no mediocrity accepted."
Mario Batali

SWEET AND SOUR SAUCE

Bellingham seems to be able to support an impressive assortment of Thai food eateries, from the student stand by, to the well-decorated-for-the-well-heeled sort of place. On Rice belongs to the latter ... In fact, you may find yourself pleasantly distracted by how lovely the place looks. From the crystal-clean fish tank that greets your eyes the moment you step in the door, to the warm colors and thoughtful, low-key decoration, On Rice somehow manages to make you feel full and cozy before you even glance at a menu - Lisa Holt

1 tsp white vinegar
½ cup ketchup
2 tsp fish sauce
4 tsp sugar
¼ cup hot water

All Thai and Asian food requires a good sweet and sour sauce. You can tell if it is freshly made, and you will find yourself putting it on everything.

1. To make the sauce, mix all the ingredients into a small glass bowl.

2. Make sure to put the hot water in last and mix with the spoon.

3. That's it...the sauce is done.

4. Remember this ingredient list is good for serving portion only. If you cook more, please double the recipe.

"...Remember fresh ingredienst can make all the difference . At On Rice we use the freshest ingredients in every dish that make our food stand out..."
Ken Tipasathien, Owner

OYSTERS BIENVILLE
AND GARDEN PARTY MARTINI

Signature Tastes of **BELLINGHAM**

Oysters Bienville:
3 dz raw oysters on the half shell
6 pie pans, filled with rock salt
4 tbsp butter
½ cup finely minced onion
½ cup minced bell pepper
1 cup minced green onion
2 cloves garlic, minced
1½ cups minced raw shrimp
1 cup mushrooms, minced
½ cup white wine
1 tbsp fresh lemon juice
2 cups Bechamel sauce
⅔ cup grated Cheddar cheese
½ cup French bread crumbs
Salt, white pepper and Tabasco to taste
Dash of Peychaud's bitters

Garden Party Martini:
1 ½ oz Hendricks Gin
½ oz Dry Vermouth
¼ oz Absinth
4 slices cucumber
3 basil leaves

Oysters Bienville

1. Preheat oven to 400°F.

2. Sauté onions, bell pepper, green onions, mushrooms and garlic in melted butter until soft; add shrimp and cook 1 minute until barely pink. Add wine and lemon juice; bring to boil.

3. Add Bechamel sauce, cheese and bread crumbs; reduce to simmer. Add salt, pepper, Tabasco and bitters. Simmer 20 minutes, or until thick.

4. Arrange 6 oysters in each pan, firmly nestled in rock salt. Cover each oyster with sauce, and bake for 10 minutes, until oysters and sauce are very hot and the top of the sauce is browned. Serve at once.

Note: the rock salt helps stabilize the oyster shells as this dish cooks. It's there for support, not seasoning; make sure you don't get any on your oysters.

Garden Party Martini

1. Muddle cucumber and basil leaves together.

2. Combine all ingredients in a shaker with ice.

3. Shake and serve up with a cucumber garnish.

Compliments of Jim Parker

OYSTER BAR AT BAYOU
1300 BAY STREET

151

CHIEF WILLIAM BOYD BELLINGHAM FIRE CHIEF

*You respond to a working fire. It's 21:00 and near-freezing outside; the building is a three-story apartment with occupants trapped. The fire extends from the first floor into an open attic area. Firefighters began their work early, and about an hour in, fire is under control, and the occupants are safe. So how do you rehab your people? With this **White Bean Chicken Chili**. "It is one of my family's favorite winter meals. Really good with fresh homemade bread." says Chief Boyd. We will test that theory on the next call...*

1 tbsp olive oil
1½ lbs boneless chicken breast
¼ cup chopped onion
1 can chicken broth
4 oz can chopped green chilis
19 oz can white kidney beans
2 green onions, chopped
1 tsp garlic powder
1 tsp ground cumin
½ tsp oregano leaves
½ tsp cilantro leaves
⅛ tsp ground red pepper

Onion and Monterey Jack cheese for garnish

1. Cut chicken breasts into small cubes.

2. Heat oil in large saucepan over med/high heat. Add chicken and onions, cook 4-5 minutes.

3. Stir in broth, chilies, spices, simmer 15 minutes.

4. Stir in beans, simmer 5 minutes.

5. Top with onions, garnish with Monterey Jack cheese.

Yields 4 cups.

PINEAPPLE FRIED RICE

Asian food is good for the soul. The origin of Chinese food therapy based on this dates back to as early as 2000 B.C. around which time the organic relationship between food property and cooking was first pointed out by Yi Yin, a slave-turned-prime-minister serving the founding Emperor of the Shang dynasty. Wok Hay - literally "Breath of the Wok," the magical moment when the energy and flavor of wok cooked food is perfectly balanced. We want you to enjoy that perfect energy, so each dish is delivered the moment it is ready.

1 lb steamed jasmine rice
4 oz frozen peas & carrots
1 pineapple, whole
1 egg, beaten in a bowl
3 stalks green onion, minced
1 tbsp sesame seeds
1 tbsp curry powder
1 tbsp turmeric
1 tbsp Thai chili paste
1 tsp red curry paste
¼ cup oyster sauce
¼ cup tomato, diced
¼ cup onions
2 sprigs basil

1. Cut a pineapple in half. Then cut the core and the meat out of it. Cut the meat portion into cubes.

2. Mix the following ingredients in a bowl and set them aside: Onions, Rice, Peas & Carrots, Curry Powder, Turmeric powder, Curry Paste, Chili Paste, Tomatoes, Basil (save 1 sprig for garnish) & Pineapple.

3. Heat & oil your wok or pan.

4. Scramble your egg then mix in your bowl of ingredients.

5. Add your oyster sauce.

6. After all ingredients are cooked into the rice serve the rice back in the hollowed out Pineapple half and garnish with Green Onions, Sesame Seeds, & Basil.

PANASIA
4876 HAXTON WAY

"…When you go to Beijing, you see what low rank you hold. When you travel to Canton, you realize how little money you've got. But when you come to Chengdu (Sichuan), you find out how large your appetite is."
Lin Yutang, My Country and My People

Pelmeni, a sort of little boiled pasties, is favorite Russian food. It's a kind of snack... you can buy them in the shops, but it's nothing comparing to home-made version. As pelmeni are kept frozen very well longtime and you can cook them quickly. Now, the Bellingham pelmeni recipe is a closely guarded secret…in fact, it is copyrighted. But the below recipe would get you a pretty good taste of it!

2 cups flour
1 cup milk
½ tsp salt
1 tbsp vegetable oil
3 eggs
½ lb beef
½ lb pork
1 onion, chopped
Salt and pepper to taste

1. Grind beef and pork twice in meat chopper. Then add chopped onion, salt and pepper.

2. To make mincemeat more tender and juicy, add a bit of milk. Reserve.

3. Mix flour with eggs and milk, salt and oil until a soft dough forms. Knead on floured surface until dough is elastic.

4. Take some dough and make a "sausage" (1" in diameter). Divide into pieces (1" thick). Roll each piece into a circle close to the size of a dumpling mold hole so that it is ¹⁄₁₆ " thick.

5. Place a dough sheet on the dumplings mold, then the filling in every opening, then cover with another dough sheet.

6. After that roll the dough circle with a rolling-pin and you have a two dozens of pelmeni at a time! Use the rest of the dough that comes out from the mold to roll another circle.

Pelmeni can be frozen to be cooked later (you can keep them in the freezer for a long time), or cooked immediately. To cook pelmeni, boil much water, so that they cannot stick to each other. Salt water. Carefully drop pelmeni into boiling water. Dont forget to stir them from time to time. Boil for 20 minutes. Pelmeni can be served with butter, sour cream, vinegar or ketchup.

"…Everything I do, I do on the principle of Russian borscht. You can throw everything into it beets, carrots, cabbage, onions, everything you want. What's important is the result, the taste of the borscht."
Yevgeny Yevtushenko, Russian poet

CILANTRO PESTO AND JICAMA SALAD

The Pepper Sisters' favorite review was written by Scott Gorman from the Everett Review and begins with a riddle "When must you go north to go southwest? When the best and most original take on a Southwestern Cuisine in some time is being served at a restaurant in this increasingly cosmopolitan university town." Pepper Sisters truly is that little piece of the Southwest in the Northwest and never disappoints, particularly if you like it spicy!

Cilantro Pesto:
4 cups chopped cilantro
¾ cup grated Romano cheese
¾ cup toasted pumpkin seeds
½ cup toasted almonds
¼ cup lemon juice
1 tsp salt
1 ½ tbsp minced garlic
½ cup olive oil

Jicama Salad:
1 medium to large jicama
½ bunch cilantro
¼ cup fresh lime juice
¼ cup salad oil
¼ tsp salt
¼ tsp cracked pepper
2 small cloves garlic, minced

Cilantro Pesto:

1. Place cilantro in food processor and pulse until minced.

2. Add all other ingredients except olive oil and process.

3. With machine running, slowly pour in olive oil to blend.

Jicama Salad:

1. Peel jicama and cut into 1/4 inch matchsticks. Place in bowl with cilantro.

2. Whisk all other ingredients together in a small bowl, then add and toss with jicama.

"...When asked if I am from the Southwest I gladly admit 'no, I am an imposter!' Truth be told, I grew up in the Hudson River Valley in New York, among a plethora of good food and good cooks...."
Susan Albert, Proprietor

SCALLOP APPETIZER

With its sleek urban décor and energetic vibe, Poppe's lush lounge is a favorite gathering place for Bellingham's happy-hour hounds. It could be the easy-on-the wallet well drinks, or the killer combination of budget friendly booze and inventive but reasonably priced nosh specials such as piping hot calamari made fresh to order or the Dungeness crab cakes.

Roasted Corn Salsa:
6 ears of corn
1 medium red onion
2 jalapenos, seeded
4 Roma tomatoes, seeded
¼ cup cilantro, chopped
1 tbsp garlic, minced
1 lime, juiced
Salt and pepper to taste

Sherry Tomato Dressing:
1 cup Sherry vinegar
1 tbsp garlic, minced
8 Roma tomatoes, cored and quartered
2 tbsp Dijon mustard
1 tsp salt
1 tsp black pepper
1 tsp dark chili powder
2 tbsp honey
¼ cup lemon juice
Pinch of dried oregano
1 cup olive oil
1 cup cilantro leaves

Scallops:
1 lb sea scallops
1 tbsp butter
Salt and pepper
1 bag mixed field greens

Roasted Corn Salsa:

1. Roast the corn with a pinch of salt and pepper until lightly charred.

2. While the corn is cooling, finely dice the onion, jalapeno and tomatoes.

3. Add then the garlic, cilantro and lime together and stir.

4. Cut the kernels of corn off of the cobs and scrape the cobs down with the back of your knife to release the corn milk.

5. Add to the salsa and set aside.

Sherry Tomato Dressing:

1. Mix together all ingredients except for the last 2 in a blender.

2. Puree until smooth then slowly add the oil to emulsify.

3. Add the cilantro at the very end and pulse a couple of times to break up the leaves.

Scallops:

1. Pan sear 1 lb of scallops dusted in salt and pepper in a hot pan with a Tablespoon of butter until caramel color starts to appear. A minute on each side should do the trick.

2. On a large platter mix 1 bag of field greens a little of the dressing, top with corn salsa, seared scallops and enjoy.

"…Why does Sea World have a seafood restaurant?? I'm halfway through my fish burger and I realize, Oh my God….I could be eating a slow learner."
Lynda Montgomery

COFFEE CRUSTED STEAK

Describing Prospect Street Café accurately can be a daunting task. Actually finding the café can also be daunting. Located directly across from the Whatcom Museum of History and Art, the café anchors the line of small businesses that rarely see evening traffic. Checking any assumptions about appearances at the door, an uncomplicated and uncompromising menu awaits. The follow recipe, developed with Emilie Stift by Chef Santenello, is an homage to the beauty of food and tastes.

(3) 3 oz beef tenderloin steaks
2 tbsp ground coffee beans
2 tbsp ground ancho chilis
4 slices bacon, cut into pieces
2 tbsp olive oil
3 tbsp sherry vinegar
2 tbsp maple syrup
2 cups spinach leaves
Smoked sea salt
Olive oil
1 egg, poached soft

1. Combine coffee and chilies to make a rub. Crust onto the steaks.

2. Grill steaks to rare (3-4 minutes per side) and set aside to rest.

3. Render bacon with olive oil until bacon is crispy over medium high heat.

4. Deglaze pan with sherry; add maple syrup.

5. Once mixture is hot, add spinach to wilt, only 30 secondsand then remove.

6. Slice steaks into slices ¼" thick, and place on spinach.

7. Sprinkle liberally with smoked sea salt and olive oil.

8. Serve with soft poached egg.

"…Chef Spencer Santenello has created a menu of 'artistry' and 'flavors with a …splendid, logical and harmonious blend…"
John Stark, The Bellingham Herald

TURKEY ARTICHOKE PANINI ON FOCCACIA

The Public Market is a year-round indoor marketplace housing a variety of local, independently owned shops and restaurants. Housing several eateries such as Juice-It!, Seven Loaves Pizzeria, Panini Grill & Deli, Schnitzel Haus, Stuart's and Makizushi, the Public Market has a myriad of tastes to offer shoppers and as a destination location in its own right.

1 focaccia loaf, split
¼ cup Dijon mustard
¼ cup mayonnaise
½ lb Gouda cheese
2 beefsteak tomatoes, sliced
1 lb smoked turkey breast, sliced
1 red onion, sliced thin
1 can artichoke hearts, roughly chopped

1. Combine mayonnaise and mustard; spread on both pieces of foccacia loaf.

2. Next add Gouda cheese to bottom loaf, then turkey.

3. Spread evenly tomatoes, onions and artichoke hearts.

4. Add top and cut into 6 sandwiches.

5. Grill for 5 minutes in a panini press.

Courtesy of Bill Simmons, Panini Grill and Deli

PUBLIC MARKET
1530 CORNWALL AVENUE

"…I went into a French restaurant and asked the waiter, 'Have you got frog's legs?' He said, 'Yes,' so I said, 'Well hop into the kitchen and get me a turkey sandwich…'."

Tommy Cooper, British entertainer and magician

CINNAMON APPLE BARS

Whether it's an intimate gathering or a grandiose celebration, every occasion is worthy of and made more memorable with amazing desserts! Each dessert is made to order, using time-honored techniques and only the freshest, most natural ingredients in each recipe. No short cuts are ever taken, nor are trans fats ever used. If you have a special request, just ask! New ideas are always welcomed and almost any craving can be accommodated!

½ cup unsalted butter, room temperature
8 oz cream cheese
2 eggs
1 cup white sugar
½ cup brown sugar
1 tbsp cinnamon
1 tbsp baking powder
½ tsp salt
1¾ cups white flour
3 apples, peeled and thinly sliced

1. Preheat oven to 350°F.

2. Prep 9"x13" pan by coating it thinly with butter and/or oil spray.

3. Mix flour, baking powder, salt and cinnamon together in a bowl – set aside.

4. Cream butter and cream cheese at medium speed until smooth.

5. Add white and brown sugar and eggs and mix at medium speed until light and fluffy.

6. Slowly incorporate flour mixture.

7. Fold in apple slices.

8. Pour into prepared baking pan and bake for 45 minutes or until a toothpick comes out clean.

9. Cool for one hour and slice then serve.

PURE BLISS DESSERTS
1424 CORNWALL AVENUE

"…These deliciously moist bars are light and fluffy with an amazing blend of sweet and tart and spice. Perfect for the fall with your favorite variety of apple…or anytime year-round."
Andi Vann, Owner

PRETZEL DUMPLING (BREZENKNOEDEL)

Ralf's started in 2003 when Ralf Sigl moved from Augsburg, Germany with his wife Kacy. One story about the origin of the Pretzel goes back to 610 A.D., when a monk took a strip of dough and formed it into the shape of a child's arms folded in prayer. He gave it as a reward to children who successfully learned their prayers, calling it a "pretiola", meaning "reward" in Latin. The pretiola became known in Germany as "Brezel," and later as "Pretzel" in America. For Ralf's, using organic ingredients is not a commitment, but a passion – combined with the ambition to make the best Bavarian Pretzel.

4 Bavarian pretzels
2 eggs
½ cup milk
1 tbsp soft butter
Handful chopped parsley
Salt and pepper

1. Bring a large pot of water or broth to boiling.

2. Cut pretzel bread into large chucks and chop into crumbs in food processor (if you don't have a food processor, cut the bread up small and let it sit with the other ingredients until the bread has softened).

3. In a bowl, beat eggs, add crumbs, milk, butter, parsley and salt and pepper. Mix well with hands, and let sit for 15 - 20 minutes.

4. With wet hands, form into balls. The size is slightly larger than a golf ball but smaller than a tennis ball.

5. Place dumpling balls into the boiling water, reduce heat, and let simmer for about 15 minutes.

Serve with thick meat or mushroom sauce. Day old dumplings taste great cut up in strips and fried in butter.

RALF'S BAKERY
207 EAST MAPLE STREET

"...I personally believe the monks invented the Pretzel to accompany their beer, a combination that has been around in the Alps for centuries..."
Ralf Sigl

SUSTAINABLE CONNECTIONS

At Sustainable Connections we love local food and the fine folks that grow and produce it. We work hard to connect our community with the plethora of local food available here in Whatcom County. Local food always makes for a better party! Please enjoy our recipe for local
Strawberry Mint Daiquiris.

10 medium to large sized farm fresh locally grown strawberries

2 sprigs fresh locally grown mint (more or less to taste)

3-4 oz dark rum

3 tbsp unrefined sugar

Crushed ice

1. Place all ingredients in blender
2. Fill blender pitcher to top with crushed ice, blend until smooth.
3. Serve with spring of mint.

For an even thicker daiquiri, freeze strawberries before using.

Makes approximately 24-28 oz.

APPLE FRITTER

Since the golden era of Doughnuts was in the 1950's & 60's, we also serve up a bit of nostalgia in our downtown bakery café. Music, Sci-fi movie trailers and original movie posters from those days transport you to a simpler time. If you are really good, the robot might even make an appearance. Take a bite and you'll agree we make them out of this world!

Fritters:
4 lbs yeast-raised dough
(recipe follows, or you can substitute frozen yeast rolls)
2½ cup cube cut apple filling
¼ cup cinnamon
1 tbsp nutmeg
Oil for frying

Glaze:
1 cup hot water
7 cups powdered sugar

Yeast-raised dough:
12 cups bread flour
4 tbsp yeast
½ cup sugar
1 tsp salt
2 cups water, lukewarm
4 tbsp butter, softened

1. Mix cinnamon and nutmeg together with apple filling.

2. Chop apple mixture into already prepared dough.

3. Use an ice cream scoop to portion into balls.

4. Slightly flatten dough onto fryer screen by using fingers (tops should be bumpy).

5. Proof the dough for 45 minutes.

6. While dough is proofing, mix together glaze and set aside.

7. Preheat deep fryer to 350°F.

8. Submerge fritters in oil for 4 ½ minutes.

9. Glaze while hot. Serve and enjoy!

Yeast-raised dough:

1. Mix water, yeast and sugar together until yeast is dissolved, about 10 minutes.

2. Mix in a mixer with a dough hook the flour, butter, salt and yeast water until dough is smooth, about 10 minutes.

3. Allow to proof (rise) for one hour or until doubled in size.

ROCKET DONUTS
306 WEST HOLLY STREET

"...Bread deals with living things, with giving life, with growth, with the seed, the grain that nurtures. It is not coincidence that we say bread is the staff of life."
Lionel Poilane

GREEK RUDY PIZZA

You'll be hard-pressed to find a pizza that offers as many possibilities as Rudy's Pizzeria, which boasts over 50 toppings on its menu. Located on State Street, Rudy's spacious interior is bright and comfortable with its cartoon-lined brick walls, vintage wooden floors and kitsch-y tables. But decisions have to be made…toppings, homemade red wine or pesto sauces and white or whole wheat crust. And you can't go wrong with any of them.

1 fresh whole wheat pizza crust
½ cup red wine marinara sauce
½ cup fresh spinach leaves
1 Roma tomato, sliced
½ red onion, sliced thin
½ cup Kalamata olives, pitted
½ cup fresh Feta cheese
1 cup mozzarella cheese
Olive oil

1. Roll out the pizza dough onto a pizza pan, about ¼" thick.

2. Preheat oven to 475°F.

3. Using the back of a ladle or spoon, spread the red wine marinara all around the pizza, to within ½" of the edge.

4. Spread all the veggies and feta cheese around the pizza, leaving no patch of sauce untouched by the toppings.

5. Add the mozzarella over all of it.

6. Bake for 8-10 minutes until bubbly, luscious and golden.

7. Allow to rest for five minutes, if you can keep your grubby mitts off of it.

"…I animated 20 years at Terry Toons. It's important to know that animators like pizza and a raise once in a while, and you've got to treat them with love."
Ralph Bakshi

WICKED MUSHROOMS

Relied upon by Scotty Brown's Restaurant & Lounge to provide their patrons an exceptional appetizer experience, the Wicked Mushroom recipe below brings Scotty Brown's fun and Asian flair to your kitchen. Your local Asian market or finer grocery store will carry the ingredients below, making this recipe an easy yet remarkable starter to a dinner party. Guaranteed to turn any house into the House of Yes.

Wicked Mushrooms:
1 oz canola oil
8 oz mushrooms
¼ oz bias cut green
onions
3 oz Wicked Sauce

Wicked Sauce:
12 oz Mirin
12 oz light soy sauce
4 oz Worcestershire
sauce
½ tbsp minced garlic
½ tsp ground pepper
½ tsp kosher salt

Wicked Sauce

1. Combine all sauce ingredients in a large pan over low heat.

2. Simmer sauce for 15 minutes.

Wicked Mushrooms:

1. In large sauté pan, heat oil over high heat.

2. Add mushrooms and sauté for 1 minute.

3. Add Wicked Mushroom Sauce to pan, and sauté for approx. 3-5 minutes.

4. Sauce should completely coat mushrooms and develop a syrupy consistency.

5. Garnish with green onions and serve hot.

"...This deceivingly simple yet elegantly flavored dish is the key to your appetizer dilemma!"
Joe Cooper, Manager

OYSTER STEW

Eighty per cent of all restaurants go bust in the first three years. Only women's clothing stores have as high a failure rate. So what does a jam-packed restaurant say about the Shrimp Shack after 27 years plus a five year absence from the already crowded restaurant market in downtown Bellingham? Something has to be pretty damn good about the place. - Glen Berry

3-5 small oysters (shucked)
½ cup heavy cream
1 cup milk
1 tbsp butter
Onion Powder
Garlic Powder
Salt
Paprika
Parsley

1. In a heavy saucepan, blanch 3 to 5 small shucked oysters in water.

2. Drain and save about ½ cup of the water in the pot.

3. Add 1 tbsp of butter to pot.

4. Add a cup of milk and cream to water.

5. Add a dash of garlic and onion powder and salt to taste.

6. Bring to boil.

7. Garnish with a bit of paprika and parsley.

8. Serve with fresh sourdough bread or soda crackers.

SHRIMP SHACK
1200 CORNWALL AVENUE

"...C'était un homme courageux qui, le premier d'ingestion e d'huîtres" (It was a brave man who first swallowed an oyster)
Wall sign in a French Creole restaurant, New Orleans

AZTEC CHICKEN LIME SOUP

Touted by many as Fairhaven's "hidden gem", Skylark's is one worth making the effort to find. Tucked away in the back of the old Fairhaven Post Office, Skylark's offers a charming, classic atmosphere – complete with it's own European style outdoor cobblestone lined eating area. Bring a hearty appetite, as one of Skylark's promises is that "we never skimp on the portion." Even their salads are a meal built for two.

1 lb chicken breast
4 stalks celery, chopped
Water to cover
4 large roma tomatoes, diced
½ medium red onion, diced
2 large jalapeño, minced
½ bunch cilantro, chopped
1 tsp garlic, minced
2 large limes

3 qt chicken stock, preferably homemade

Tortilla chips or warm flour tortillas

1. Cut chicken into 1" cubes then place in medium saucepan. Add chopped celery and enough water to cover by about one inch. Bring to boil and continue to boil for approximately 30 minutes or until tender enough to shred with a fork. Remove chicken from cooking liquid. Discard liquid and celery.

2. Shred chicken into small bowl and refrigerate.

3. Clean and cut vegetables as listed. The proper dice is small like in a salsa and the jalapeño should be minced very, very small. Place in small bowl and toss with fork to combine. Refrigerate.

4. Cut limes into 8 wedges each and refrigerate in another small bowl.

5. Combine garlic and chicken stock in medium saucepan. Bring to boil, then reduce heat and keep very hot.

To serve, put 2 tbsp of vegetable mixture and 1 tbsp shredded chicken into soup cup (double for a bowl). Ladle hot chicken stock over vegetables. Squeeze juice of one lime wedge (two for a bowl). Serve with tortilla chips or warm flour tortillas.

SKYLARK'S HIDDEN CAFÉ
1308 11TH STREET

"...He who distinguishes the true savor of his food can never be a glutton; he who does not cannot be otherwise..."
Henry David Thoreau

CRAB DIP

Elegant dining in an intimate atmosphere…the Steak House offers specially selected & naturally aged Prime Steaks for maximum tenderness & flavor. Broiled at 1800 degrees and basted with steak butter before serving, our steaks are sensational. They offer an extensive wine list and delectable desserts.

20 oz crab, thawed and drained
3 lb cream cheese
¾ lb roasted red pepper, diced
1 cup green onion, chopped
4 tsp dried basil
4 tsp dried mustard
4 tsp paprika
1 tsp cayenne pepper

1. Soften the cream cheese for several hours.
2. In a mixer, add all other ingredients.
3. Mix well, scrape the bowl a few times to thoroughly combine.
4. Refrigerate overnight to allow the flavors to meld.
5. Serve with sourdough bread toast points.

STEAK HOUSE AT SILVER REEF
4876 HAXTON WAY

"…A bath and a tenderloin steak. Those are the high points of a man's life. "
Curt Siodmak, novelist and screenwriter

PAPAYA SALAD

This green papaya salad, known as som tam, is popular in most areas of Thailand, and when you taste it, you'll know why. The slightly tart flavor of the green papaya combines well with the spice of red chili pepper and the saltiness of shrimp paste and fish sauce, plus the sweetness of honey. Green papaya salad is a beautifully unique and flavor-filled dish that will make a great impression. It's also easy to make, low-calorie, and very nutritious. So try this Som tam recipe for dinner tonight!

1 small green papaya, or ½ large (your papaya should be very firm, the flesh white to light orange in color)
½ cup roasted peanuts
½ cup green beans, bias cut
1 to 2 tomatoes, cut into long thin strips
1 red chili, minced
3 spring onions, sliced into long matchstick-like pieces
½ cup fresh basil, roughly chopped if leaves are large
Handful of fresh coriander

Dressing:
½ tsp shrimp paste
2 tbsp good-tasting oil, such as olive
2 tbsp fish sauce
3 tbsp lime juice

1. Prepare the dressing by mixing together all dressing ingredients together in a cup. Make sure shrimp paste and honey dissolve fully. Set aside.

2. Peel the green papaya, then slice it in half and remove all the seeds. Using the largest grater you have, grate the papaya (or you can use a potato peeler to create thin, ribbon-like strips). Place in a large bowl.

3. Add the sliced tomato, spring onion, chili, bean sprouts, and most of the basil. Add the dressing, tossing to combine.

4. Add the peanuts (you can either leave them whole, or roughly chop them). Toss again. Taste-test the salad. If not sweet enough, add a little more honey. If not salty enough, add a little more fish sauce. If too sweet or salty, add more lime juice. If you prefer it spicier, add more fresh-cut chili or dried crushed chili.

5. To serve, scoop the salad into individual bowls or onto a serving platter. Sprinkle with remaining basil leaves plus fresh coriander. Serve immediately and enjoy!

"...Looking for peace is like looking for a turtle with a mustache: You won't be able to find it. But when your heart is ready, peace will come looking for you..."
Ajahn Chah (Thai buddhist, 1918-1992)

DAVID TRAYNOR WINEMAKER, MOUNT BAKER VINEYARDS

*The wine business is, above all else, about food, family, friends, and the joy of entertaining! Whenever my family entertains, or attends gatherings at other homes, it seems that we are always asked if these **Stuffed Mushrooms** will be there. It is a family affair in the kitchen with this recipe. Even my six year old son has a job to do! We have been using this recipe for 5 years now, and my wife's parents used it long before that. Pair with a full bodied, local, white wine, and enjoy!*

24 medium mushrooms, about 1 lb
6 tbsp margarine or butter
1 small onion, chopped
¼ tsp garlic powder, or 2 cloves garlic, minced
1 (3-ounce) package low-fat cream cheese, softened
3 tbsp grated Parmesan
2 tbsp chopped fresh parsley leaves, or 2 tsp dried parsley flakes
1 cup packaged herb-seasoned stuffing croutons

1. Preheat oven to 425°F.

2. Remove stems from mushrooms. Chop enough stems to make 1 cup.

3. Melt 2 tbsp of margarine or butter in saucepan. Brush mushroom cap tops with margarine, place top side down in shallow baking pan and brush undersides of caps.

4. Heat remaining margarine in same saucepan. Add chopped mushroom stems, onion and garlic and cook until tender.

5. Stir in cream cheese, combining with fork if necessary.

6. Add Parmesan cheese, parsley and herb seasoned stuffing. Mix thoroughly.

7. Spoon about 1 tbsp of stuffing mixture into each mushroom cap.

8. Bake until heated through.

   Tip: To make ahead, prepare as directed but do not bake. Cover and refrigerate up to 24 hours. Bake as directed.

Signature Tastes of BELLINGHAM

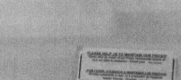

TOMATO RED SAUCE WITH CORN TORTILLAS

If you like authentic style, you'll like Taco Lobo. Don't expect American-style mexican. Your taco will not be a hard greasy bright yellow shell with ground beef and cheddar cheese, lettuce and tomatoes, but rather shredded chicken, pork or steak with cilantro, onions and cabbage. The best part is the homemade corn tortillas and the salsa bar. This is one of the sauces on that bar.

5 medium Roma tomatoes, ripe
1 jalapeno chili, large
2 tbsp fresh oregano
Salt to taste

Corn Tortillas:
1¾ cups masa harina
1⅛ cups water

Sauce:

1. Blend all ingredients in a blender on high for 1 minute.

2. Taste and adjust salt.

3. Blend again for 1 minute.

4. Store in refrigerator overnight to allow flavours to develop.

Tortillas:

1. In a medium bowl, mix together masa harina and hot water until thoroughly combined. Turn dough onto a clean surface and knead until pliable and smooth. If dough is too sticky, add more masa harina; if it begins to dry out, sprinkle with water. Cover dough tightly with plastic wrap and allow to stand for 30 minutes.

2. Preheat a cast iron skillet or griddle to medium-high.

3. Divide dough into 15 equal-size balls. Using a tortilla press, a rolling pin, or your hands, press each ball of dough flat between two sheets of plastic wrap.

4. Immediately place tortilla in preheated pan and allow to cook for approximately 30 seconds, or until browned and slightly puffy. Turn tortilla over to brown on second side for approximately 30 seconds more, then transfer to a plate. Repeat process with each ball of dough. Keep tortillas covered with a towel to stay warm and moist until ready to serve.

TACO LOBO
117 WEST MAGNOLIA STREET

"...The salsa selection is great, too and it's all home-made..."
TripAdvisor.com

SAZERAC

The signature cocktail of The Temple Bar, the Sazerac, is reported to be the first cocktail invented in the United States and Antoine Amadie Peychaud, is credited. In 1795, he opened a drugstore called Pharmacie Peychaud in New Orleans. Like many "chemists" of his day, he sold his own patent medicine; Peychaud's Bitters, a mix of aromatic bitters said to relive ailments. Invented in 1830, his medical toddy soon became very popular. No wonder The Temple Bar is deemed as one of the best places to recharge in Bellingham.

½ tsp of absinthe
1 sugar cube
Peychaud's Bitters
2½ oz rye whiskey
1 large strip lemon zest

1. Coat the inside of a small glass with absinthe.

2. In a pint glass, saturate a sugar cube with Peychaud's Bitters.

3. Add a little ice and the rye whiskey to the pint glass.

4. Stir the rye, ice, bitters/sugar gently.

5. Strain into the absinthe-rinsed glass.

6. Zest a large strip of lemon peel over the glass. This ensures the oils from the lemon peel will fall into the drink. Rub the zest around the edge of glass, if you like.

7. Drop the lemon zest into your drink.

Note: the amount of bitters and absinthe depends entirely on you. Experiment with the portions to get the Sazerac you desire!

"...If more of us valued food and cheer and song above hoarded gold, it would be a merrier world..."
J. R. R. Tolkien

VEGAN TOFU GUMBO

Signature Tastes of BELLINGHAM

1 qt water
2 tbsp veggie base
½ brick tofu
2 tbsp margarine
2 tbsp flour
1 onion
2 stalks celery
¾ green pepper
¼ red pepper
2 scallions
½ cup rice

Spices:
¼ tsp cayenne pepper
¼ tsp black pepper
½ tsp salt
¾ tsp oregano
2 tbsp garlic

1. Whisk together your water and veggie base and get simmering.

2. Cut your tofu brick and lay on cookie sheet in between towels and press for at least 20 mins under a heavy item (for example a bean bag).

3. Chop your veggies.

4. Over low heat in a saute pan, start your roux, melt margarine and let it simmer till its frothy. Slowly whisk in flour and veggie base (dissolved in hot water). Whisk in all spices except garlic.

5. Add your veggies to your roux and cook over low heat, covered. Be careful to not burn.

6. Chop your tofu into bite-sized chunks. Coat w/a little olive oil and a little pinch of each of your spices and bake on a cookie sheet for 20 minutes or until golden brown.

7. Cook your rice, strain and add to soup. When your sauté has about 5 minutes left, add your garlic (minced or chopped up in a cuisinart).

9. Add your finished sauté and tofu to soup.

10. Taste, adjust, and enjoy!

Note: a sauté cooked in roux takes much longer to cook than other sautés. Make sure your veggies aren't too crunchy and don't burn your roux.

THE BAGELRY
1319 RAILROAD AVENUE

"An old-fashioned vegetable soup, without any enhancement, is a more powerful anticarcinogen than any known medicine..."
James Duke M.D.(U.S.D.A.)

BUTTERMILK SCONE

Rockin' breakfast and better lunch. Made from scratch pastries, soups, salads, stone fire pizzas and calzones, organic free trade Tony's Coffee, espresso and fantastic free range organic eggs! Fun waitstaff and open kitchen so you can watch the cooks flip eggs.

2 ¼ cups all-purpose flour
½ tsp salt
1 tbsp baking powder
½ tsp baking soda
6 tbsp unsalted butter
(warmed but not melted)

¾ cups buttermilk
(½ now ¼ for glazing)
2 eggs
4 tbsp lightly packed brown sugar
2 tsp vanilla
(maybe a dash more)
4 raw sugar packets

1. In a bowl whisk together ½ cup of buttermilk, whole egg, the brown sugar, and the vanilla till there are no more lumps.

2. In another bowl add flour, baking powder and baking soda and lightly mix together

3. Nuke your butter for 10-15 seconds or until soft but not melted, then blend the butter using a pastry tool until it resembles coarse meal.

4. Pour your flour mixture into your wet mixture and slowly stir together until combined.

5. Knead dough gently forming into a round ball. Squish down and start to form a circle with your hands until the whole thing sits about 1" to 1½" thick and about 8" in diameter.

6. Take your last egg and separate the yolk and discard. Add ¼ cup of buttermilk to egg white and whisk till combined. Spread very thinly over top of dough and sprinkle 4 packets of raw sugar evenly over top.

7. Cut into 8 pieces and place on cookie sheet with parchment paper. Place in a 350°F oven for 8 minutes or until slightly raised and golden brown.

8. Take out and let scones cool for at least 10 minutes, then cut down middle with bread knife making sure not to cut all the way through. Fill with raspberry jam, spreading evenly throughout center with a knife (tricky but do-able) and enjoy.

"...You are making me fat, but I still love you. I ate you for dinner tonight and last night. You are good old and young. You are sticky in the morning when I put you out to sell. I gave one of you to a homeless man in front of Whole Foods. He loved you too..."
Julia Doctoroff, "Ode to a Scone"

COTTAGE CAKES WITH BERRY COMPOTE

The Fork at Agate Bay is a cyclist owned and operated restaurant that specializes in delicious food, beer and wine. The environment is relaxed and so are the people, which create the perfect after ride spot to grab beers and food with the family. John and Gina Russell strike a perfect balance between exciting entrees with casual comfort. With a constantly changing menu, the Fork is always leaving people surprised and satisfied, which creates a haven for the local food and wine connoisseur.

Cottage Cakes:
4 cups flour
1 cup sugar
2 tbsp baking powder
½ tbsp baking soda
1 tsp salt
8 eggs, separated
4 cups half & half
3 cups cottage cheese
1 tbsp vanilla
½ pound butter, melted

Berry Compote:
1 pint strawberries
2 pints blackberries
2 pints blueberries
1 cup apple juice
1 cup orange juice
Juice and zest of 3 lemons
1 tsp cardamom (strong flavor, optional)
3 tsp cinnamon
1 tsp nutmeg
1 tsp ginger powder
3 cups sugar

Cottage Cakes:

1. Whisk together dry ingredients in medium bowl.

2. In separate bowl whisk egg whites until stiff.

3. Fold in Half & Half, Cottage Cheese, Egg Yolks, and Vanilla.

4. Whisk in dry ingredients.

5. Add melted butter and stir until combined.

6. Ladle large spoonfuls onto a greased hot griddle.

7. Top with Berry Compote or serve on the side!

Berry Compote:

1. Put all ingredients in to large (6 qt approx) saucepot.

2. Cook over medium heat until fruit is tender.

3. Strain and put liquid back on heat. Keep fruit in separate bowl.

4. Reduce liquid by ½.

5. Add back to fruit.

"…The laziest man I ever met put popcorn in his pancakes so they would turn over by themselves."
W. C. Fields

MATTIE'S CRAZY AVOCADO

A coffeehouse, a cafe, a grand cafe, a wine bar, a village pub, a bottle shop, a French bistro, and an American diner. The Fountain is whatever you are. The Fountain is whatever you need. Thoughtful, attentive, and reasonable, The Fountain will satisfy your conscience, and flatter your pocket. Much like the proverbial fountain of yore, The Fountain will provide nourishment from dawn until late to our neighbors near and far.

Filling:
1 tub chevre
3 tbsp dried basil
3 tbsp dried thyme
3 tbsp fresh parsley
2 oz lemon juice
1 tbsp Tabasco
Salt and pepper to taste
4 tbsp minced garlic

Avocado:
1 baguette sliced into ¼ inch pieces, slightly toasted
2 avocados, halved and pit removed
½ cup shredded Parmesan

Filling:

1. Mix chevre and all other filling ingredients together in a bowl.

2. Place ¼ cup in each halved avocado.

3. Put 2 tbsp of parmesan cheese over each avocado.

4. Place in 450°F oven for 7 minutes.

5. Remove from oven and serve immediately with toasted bread pieces.

THE FOUNTAIN BISTRO
1910 BROADWAY

"...One of my good friends and co-worker "Mattie" came up with this one. I thought it sounded crazy enough to work and it does..It goes great spread over toasted bread or just about anything else you can imagine..."
Ott Statzel, Kitchen Manager

BAKER HIGH APPLE PIE

We opened The Grace Café in August 2000 with a passion for pies and a commitment to customer service. Handmade, New York-style bagels were already a staple of the business and continue to be an anchor of The Grace Café. We have since added many other handcrafted made-from-scratch, baked goods to our menu. Gigantic muffins, enormous gooey cinnamon rolls, fruit-filled scones, huge cookies, and handmade pies are just some of the goodies you'll find.

Favorite double crust recipe
3 lbs Granny Smith or Gravenstein Apples, peeled, cored & sliced.
1 tbsp lemon juice
½ cup sugar
3 tbsp corn starch
¼ tsp salt
½ tsp nutmeg
½ tsp cinnamon

1. Prepare your pie crust recipe. You may need more than standard amount due to the height of the apples. We can't give our recipe out as it is a closely guarded secret!

2. Toss apples in approximately 1 tsp lemon juice to prevent browning.

3. Combine the dry ingredients and toss the dry ingredients with the apples.

4. Place apple mixture in bottom shell of pie crust, mounding them "Baker" high. Dot the apples with butter.

5. Lay the top crust over the mound of apples and crimp the edges until pretty!

6. Put several small slits in top crust to release the moisture during baking. Pre-heat oven to 425°F.

7. Bake pie for 50 minutes then reduce heat to 350°F and continue baking for 10-20 minutes.

8. Insert a knife through the center of the crust to test the tenderness of the apples. Some people prefer crisp, some prefer soft.

Note: You may want to have a drip pan underneath when baking.

THE GRACE CAFÉ
1065 EAST SUNSET DRIVE

"But I, when I undress me
Each night, upon my knees
Will ask the Lord to bless me
With apple-pie and cheese."
Eugene Field, 'Apple-Pie and Cheese'

STRAWBERRY RHUBARB COMPOTE

For over ten years The Mount Bakery in downtown Bellingham has produced award winning scratch baked pastries, cakes, and other desserts while also providing a delicious breakfast and lunch to their cafe customers. This strawberry rhubarb compote is one of many seasonal offerings the bakery makes featuring locally sourced and organic ingredients.

2 lbs local organic rhubarb* washed and cut into ½ inch pieces

1 pint local organic strawberries* washed and quartered

*(both available from our friend Helen of Sumas River Farm at the Saturday Farmers' Market)

¾ cup sugar
½ tsp ground ginger
¼ cup orange juice
½ of a vanilla bean split length wise
pinch of salt

Compote:

1. Combine all ingredients except strawberries in a medium saucepan.

2. Cook over medium low heat stirring occasionally until rhubarb is soft but not falling apart (approx. 8 to 10 minutes).

3. Remove from heat.

4. Find and discard vanilla bean husk.

5. Stir in strawberries. Berries will be cooked by residual heat.

6. Enjoy served atop a Belgian waffle with a medium scoop of Mallard Super Vanilla ice cream.

Recipe by Elizabeth Ruth at the Mount Bakery.

THE MOUNT BAKERY
308 C WEST CHAMPION STREET

"...Mount Bakery loves the Bellingham Farmer's Market!! Great vendors, great music and entertainment, and sweet market staff..."
Vincent Lalonde , Owner

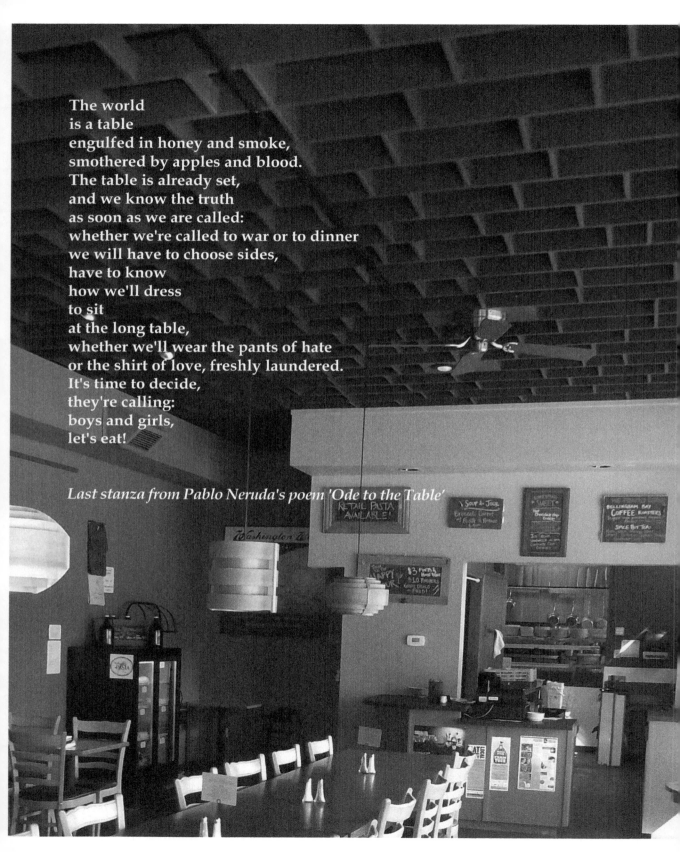

The world
is a table
engulfed in honey and smoke,
smothered by apples and blood.
The table is already set,
and we know the truth
as soon as we are called:
whether we're called to war or to dinner
we will have to choose sides,
have to know
how we'll dress
to sit
at the long table,
whether we'll wear the pants of hate
or the shirt of love, freshly laundered.
It's time to decide,
they're calling:
boys and girls,
let's eat!

Last stanza from Pablo Neruda's poem 'Ode to the Table'

CREAMY SAGE PUMPKIN PASTA

The founders of the Bellingham Pasta Company believe that no neighborhood, town or county should be without a fresh pasta provider. This recipe was featured at the Bellingham Farmers Market "Squash Smack Down". Using fresh pasta, sage and pumpkin really make this dish come alive. And kids love it!

1 lb fresh penne pasta
1½ tablespoon olive oil
1 small onion or shallot
2 cloves of garlic, minced
1 cup chicken broth
½ cup white wine
1½ cup diced pumpkin
½ cup heavy cream
2 tbsp chopped fresh sage
¾ teaspoon salt
½ ground pepper
¼ tsp ground nutmeg
½ cup grated parmesan cheese

1. Bring a large pot of salted water to boil for the pasta.

2. Meanwhile, heat olive oil over medium heat in large skillet, add onions and garlic. Cook until tender, about 5 minutes.

3. Add fresh pumpkin and broth to mixture and cook until tender about 3 minutes.

4. Mash pumpkin with potato masher. Add heavy cream, sage, nutmeg, salt and pepper and heat though.

5. Cook fresh pasta in boiling water for 3 minutes, then transfer to skillet with the pumpkin sauce and serve warm.

6. Top with cheese and serve.

Pair with Pinot Noir.

Signature Tastes of BELLINGHAM

THE TABLE BY BELLINGHAM PASTA CO.
100 NORTH COMMERCIAL STREET

"Everything you see I owe to pasta." Sophia Loren
"Life is a combination of magic and pasta." Federico Fellini
Requoted by Katie Hinton, Nikki Williamson and Anna Rankin, Co-owners

MEAT CALZONE

Calzone basically translates to "pocket or trouser sandwich" (no comments on that one, people). What better way to enjoy some of Italy's finest delicacies than all in one sandwich? The great thing about this, is once it is cooked, you can serve it warm (not hot). Owner Carl Freeman cannot part with his recipe for pizza dough or marinara, but the home chef can easily use their own recipe to make this delicious meal for two.

Fresh made pizza dough
4 oz ricotta cheese
½ cup mozzarella, shredded
1 tbsp parmesan cheese
4 slices Canadian bacon
4 slices pepperoni, large
½ cup Italian sausage, browned
¼ cup bacon, fried and diced
Marinara Sauce
4 tbsp butter, melted
4 cloves garlic, diced

1. Roll out dough until thin, about ⅛" thick.

2. Dot ricotta over dough, spreading flat with a knife.

3. Spread ½ of mozzarella and parmesan over ½ of dough. This will form the bottom of the calzone.

4. In this order, add the meat:
   a. Canadian bacon
   b. Pepperoni
   c. Italian sausage
   d. Bacon

5. Top with ¼ to ½ cup of marinara sauce.

6. Add remaining cheeses to top of marinara.

7. Fold over the half of dough without toppings.

8. Roll edge of doughs together to ensure the calzone is sealed.

9. Cut two slits in top to vent steam.

10. Combine butter and garlic, and baste entire calzone.

11. Bake for 8 minutes at 500ºF.

"...The former owner of a Palm Coast pizzeria accused of attacking customers who complained about their [calzone] order, has been sentenced to 10 years in prison..." (A chef takes his calzone seriously!)

News excerpt from the Palm Beach Post newspaper

CAPRICE TESKE DIRECTOR, BELLINGHAM FARMER'S MARKET

*This dish (**Vegan Mushroom Pate**) is the perfect appetizer to suit all different dietary needs and tastes. It is one of my favorite items to take to parties and you can dress it up (form it in a loaf pan for an elegant presentation) or down (simply pile it in a crock for spreading). It is also great as a hearty spread on a sandwich or a filling for an omelette.*

2 tbsp olive oil
3 tbsp minced shallots
2 cups finely chopped wild mushrooms (shiitake, porcini, portobello)
½ cup finely chopped parsley
¼ teaspoon dried thyme
¼ cup cooking sherry

Onion and Monterey Jack cheese for garnish

1. Heat olive oil in a medium skillet over medium-high heat.

2. Add the shallots; cook, stirring, until softened, about 1 minute.

3. Add the mushrooms and sherry; cook, stirring until softened, about 5 minutes.

4. Continue cooking until all liquid has evaporated.

5. Stir in the parsley and thyme; cook, stirring, 30 seconds.

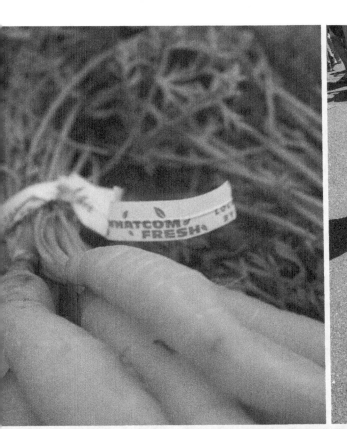

COQ AU VIN

Until the 20th century it was common for rural families in France to keep chickens and a rooster. The rooster would be kept until it was too old to perform its duties, at which time it would be eaten. However, by this time the meat would be hard and stringy, so cooking it slowly in wine would tend to soften the meat and make it more edible. As such, the recipe has historically been considered "peasant food" or "poor people's food" as the well-off would be able to afford a better cut of meat which would not require slow cooking in wine in order to be edible. This is a recipe from Chef Nate and Kelly Becklund from Tivoli French Bistro.

Marinade:
4 leg/thigh quarter chicken
2 carrots (rough chop)
2 ribs of celery (rough chop)
1 onion (rough chop)
4 cloves of garlic (whole)
1 small bunch of fresh thyme
Parsley stems
2 bay leaves
4 whole peppercorns
Red wine to cover
Flour
Salt and pepper

Sauce:
1 tbsp unsalted butter
¼ lb thick cut bacon
3 cups button mushrooms
1½ cup of pearl onions
1 whole onion (small dice)
2 ribs of celery (small dice)
2 carrots (small dice)
½ cup of port wine

1. Mix together all ingredients in the marinade, place in a container for 24 hours.

2. After 24 hours, pull chicken out of marinade and set on a rack and pat really dry. Reserve marinade. Salt and pepper chicken, then dust with flour.

3. Cut bacon into 1/4 inch slices crosswise. Cut off mushroom stems, quarter cap. Blanch onions in boiling salted water, shock in ice water, peel off skin.

4. In a braising pot, cover bottom surface with canola oil and heat. When oil begins to smoke, sear chicken fat side down till brown, then flip.

5. Pour in reserved marinade and bring to a boil. Turn down to a simmer for 45 minutes. Skim fat and foam.

6. Cool chicken in braising liquid completely. This prevents chicken from drying out. Take chicken out and set aside. Strain braising liquid through mesh strainer and reserve.

7. In another pot, add butter and bacon and render out. Add mirepoix (carrots, celery, onion), salt and pepper, and sweat out till clear.

8. Add mushrooms and stir. Add port wine to deglaze the pot, then strained braising liquid. Bring to a boil, then turn down to a simmer. Skim fat and foam.

9. Add pearl onions and chicken. Simmer till mirepoix is tender and you are done!

This dish goes well with egg noodles, mash potatoes, or we like to serve it with spaetzle.

"…I want there to be no peasant in my kingdom so poor that he cannot have a chicken in his pot every Sunday…"
King Henry IV

IRISH CAR BOMB

David and Molly met in New York City while working at an Irish Pub together. They soon fell in love. One thing led to the next and they ended up on the west coast where they worked in Irish bars in San Francisco and Seattle before coming to Bellingham, opening Uisce on St. Patrick's Day 2006. They love Bellingham and feel blessed to live in and own a business in such an amazing community.

½ oz Irish Cream (Bailey's)
½ pint Stout (Guinness)
½ oz Irish Whiskey (Jameson)

1. Pour half a pint of chilled Guinness into a beer mug and let it settle.

2. Take a shot glass filled with ½ oz of Irish whiskey on the bottom and ½ oz of Irish cream on top.

3. Drop the shot glass into the Guinness and chug.

"…Irish Whiskey = uisce beatha ("Water of Life" in Gaelic) It doesn't really matter by what name you call it Irish Whiskey is one of those fine things in life which requires the need for you to partake in order to determine for yourself just what all the fuss is about… "

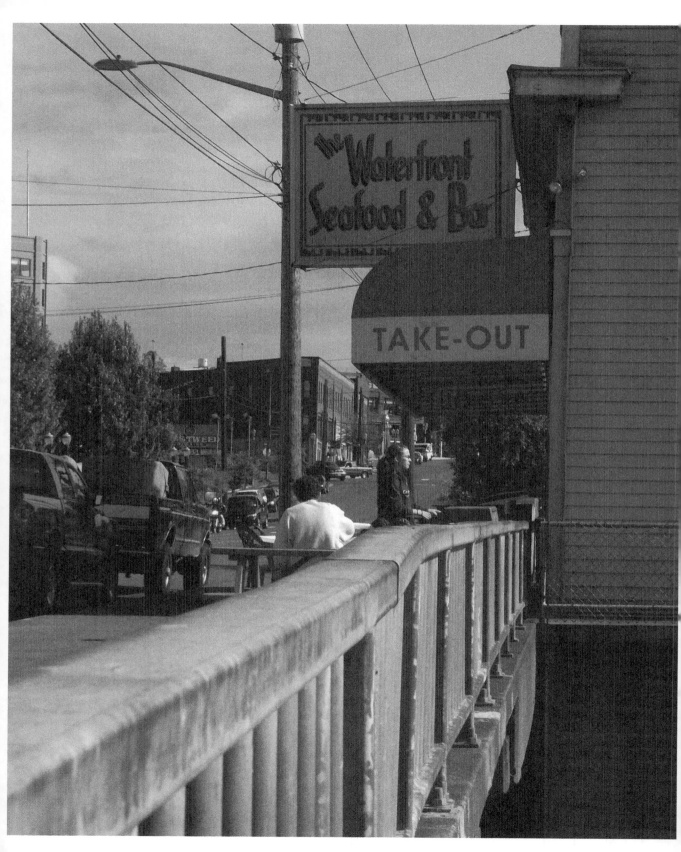

CLAM CHOWDER

1 celery stalk
¼ med onion
2 slices bacon, chopped
2 potatoes, cubed
(2) 10 oz cans chopped clams
(1) 10 oz can clam juice
1 tsp garlic powder
2 tbsp clam base
½ tsp white pepper
½ tsp thyme
1 tbsp lemon juice
2 cups half & half

1. Sauté celery onion and bacon.

2. Add potatoes, clams, clam juice, garlic powder, clam base, white pepper, thyme and lemon juice.

3. Bring to boil. Reduce and add half & half. Simmer until potatoes are done.

4. Thicken with a thickening agent (cook equal parts flour and butter together).

Signature Tastes of **BELLINGHAM**

WATERFRONT TAVERN
521 WEST HOLLY STREET

"But when that smoking chowder came in, the mystery was delightfully explained. Oh! sweet friends, hearken to me. It was made of small juicy clams, scarcely bigger than hazel nuts, mixed with pounded ship biscuits and salted pork cut up into little flakes! the whole enriched with butter, and plentifully seasoned with pepper and salt.....we dispatched it with great expedition."
Herman Melville - Ishmael in 'Moby Dick' (1851)

LAMB MOUSSAKA

Anchoring the community of higher education, Western Washington University is home to over 14,000 students. And what do you feed these perpetually hungry students? Well, that task falls to Ira Simon and the rest of the staff of University Dining. If the following recipe is any indication of the foodstuffs that students enjoy, I think we all might be well served to consider the benefits of higher education.

Eggplant:
3 large eggplants, peeled, sliced ¼ inch thick
Kosher salt
Italian vinaigrette

Lamb meat sauce:
1¼ cups ¼" diced onion
¾ cup ¼"diced celery
¼ cup sliced garlic
1 tsp each dry basil, oregano and thyme
1 oz oil blend
2 tbsp butter
½ tsp each: cinnamon, cardamom & cumin
¼ tsp each: ground clove, coriander & allspice
1 lb ground lamb
1 tsp each salt and pepper
¼ cup sun dried tomatoes, very finely minced
6 oz tomato sauce
½ cup red cooking wine, flamed
2 eggs, mixed well

Alfredo sauce:
1 cup heavy cream
1 cup real parmesan
1 tsp salt
¼ tsp white pepper
1 tbsp granulated garlic
1 lg egg, mixed

Eggplant:
1. Sprinkle generously with kosher salt on both sides and let sit for 30 minutes. The eggplant will sweat considerably. Rinse the moisture and the salt completely off of the eggplant slices, then tamp dry with paper towels or a clean cloth.
2. Marinate the slices overnight in your favorite Italian, balsamic or sundried tomato vinaigrette, then grill or bake until tender. Cool immediately. Set aside.

Lamb meat sauce:
1. Sauté until vegetables become translucent. Add remaining spices and sauté one minute.
2. Add lamb, salt and pepper and sauté until lamb is fully cooked.
3. Add tomatoes sauce and wine and simmer 10 minutes.
4. Cool. Add 2 eggs, mix well.

Alfredo sauce:
1. Mix first three ingredients well over a low heat. Simmer and stir in cheese, salt & pepper.. Simmer 5 minutes, stirring constantly.
2. Strain & cool. Whisk in one large egg.

Assembly:
1. In a 9"x12" pan, layer :⅓ eggplant, half of the lamb sauce, ½ cup shredded parmesan, ⅓ eggplant, the rest of lamb sauce, ½ cup shredded parmesan, ⅓ eggplant, 1½ cups garlic alfredo/egg mixture.
2. Bake covered at 300°F for 45 minutes.
3. Uncover, sprinkle with parmesan and breadcrumbs, bake 10 more minutes.

This recipe can easily scale up to a 5 times recipe for a large batch, or make extra meat sauce and freeze it. The lamb sauce is also excellent served over pasta.

"...I don't like gourmet cooking or "this" cooking or "that" cooking. I like good cooking...."
James Beard

COCONUT CREAM ICED MOCHA

The Woods Coffee was established in 2002 by the Herman family of Lynden. With a dream of starting a chain of coffee shops, the family pooled their talents and resources to create the first store at Bender Plaza in Lynden. Six months later, they opened their second store, and have continued on a steady growth pattern throughout Whatcom County. So like the song says, "...everybody raise your coffee in the air and say 'Yeah...'."

10 oz whole milk
1 tbsp white chocolate sauce
1½ tbsp coconut syrup
2oz (2 shots) of Espresso
Ice
Whipped cream (Optional)

1. Pour 10 oz whole milk into a 16 oz glass. .

2. Add White Chocolate Sauce, Coconut Syrup, 2 oz Espresso and stir well.

3. Top with ice and whipped cream.

THE WOODS COFFEE
MULTIPLE BELLINGHAM LOCATIONS

"...We give of ourselves in many different ways in this community, so we are really tied to the community. We have become the local, community-driven coffee shop and we work hard at every single detail..."
Wes Herman, Owner

Big Daddy restaurant at 501 W. Holly Street. c 1964

Steven W. Siler is a firefighter-cum-chef serving in Bellingham, Washington. Long marinated in the epicurean heritage of the Deep South, Steven has spent over 20 years (dear God has it been that long?!) in the much-vaulted restaurant industry from BOH to FOH to chef. In addition, he has served as an editor and contributing writer for several food publications. When not trying to shove food down his fellow firefighters' gullets, he enjoys sailing and sampling the finest of scotches and wines, and has an irrational love

affair with opera. He swears one day he will relive the above picture on the Gulf Coast with a good Will.

SMOKE ALARM

The Signature Tastes of Bellingham is the first of a series of culinary celebrations from Smoke Alarm Media, based in the Pacific Northwest. Smoke Alarm Media is named for another series of unfortunate culinary accidents at an unnamed fire department, also in the Pacific Northwest. One of the founders was an active firefighter. Having been trained as a chef, he found himself in the position of cooking frequently at the fire station. Alas, his culinary skills were somewhat lacking in using the broiler and smoke would soon fill the kitchen and station. The incidents became so frequent that the 911 dispatch would call the station and ask if "Chef Smoke Alarm" would kindly refrain from cooking on his shift. Thus Smoke Alarm Media was born.